Contents

Roy Rogers 1999, 8½" x 11" print by artist Jeffery Fain, print $75.00, original art $250.00.

Roy Rogers AND Dale Evans

TOYS & MEMORABILIA

IDENTIFICATION & VALUES

P. Allan Coyle

COLLECTOR BOOKS

A Division of Schroeder Publishing Co., Inc.

The current values in this book should be used only as a guide. They are not intended to set prices, which vary from one section of the country to another. Auction prices as well as dealer prices vary greatly and are affected by condition and demand. Neither the author nor the publisher assumes responsibility for any losses which might be incurred as a result of consulting this guide.

ON THE COVER

Front: 8½" plaster lamp with engraved Roy Rogers & Trigger signature with original shade, c. 1950s. C10–$450.00, C8–$300.00, C6–$150.00; deduct $100.00 if missing original shade.
Roy Rogers, Dale Evans & Trigger, Post Grape Nut Cereals Buttons, c. 1950s. Roy Rogers: C10–$40.00, C8–$25.00, C6–$15.00; Dale Evans or Trigger: C10–$20.00, C8–$12.00, C6–$8.00.
Roy Rogers 8½" ranch lantern by Ohio Art, c. 1950s. C10–$200.00, C8–$100.00, C6–$50.00; add $250.00 for box.
Roy Rogers and Dale Evans lunchbox & thermos by American Thermos, 1957. C10–$425.00, C8–$250.00, C6–$75.00.

Back: Roy Rogers black felt cowboy hat, c. 1950s. C10–$100.00, C8–$60.00, C6–$25.00.
Roy Rogers & Trigger tin litho wall bank by Ohio Art, c. 1950s. C10–$250.00, C8–$150.00, C6–$75.00; add $50 for original lock and key; add $100.00 for original package.
Roy Rogers, Dale Evans & Dusty boxed Junior Jigsaw Puzzle, c. 1950s. C10–$50.00, C8–$35.00, C6–$20.00.
Roy Rogers carded 9" Kilgore Cap Gun, c. 1950s. C10–$200.00, C8–$125.00, C6–$50.00; add $125.00 for rack card.

Cover design: Beth Summers
Book design: Holly C. Long

Searching For A Publisher?

We are always looking for knowledgeable people considered experts within their fields. If you feel that there is a real need for a book on your collectible subject and have a large comprehensive collection, contact Collector Books.

Collector Books

P.O. Box 3009

Paducah, KY 42002-3009

www.collectorbooks.com

Copyright © 2000 by P. Allan Coyle

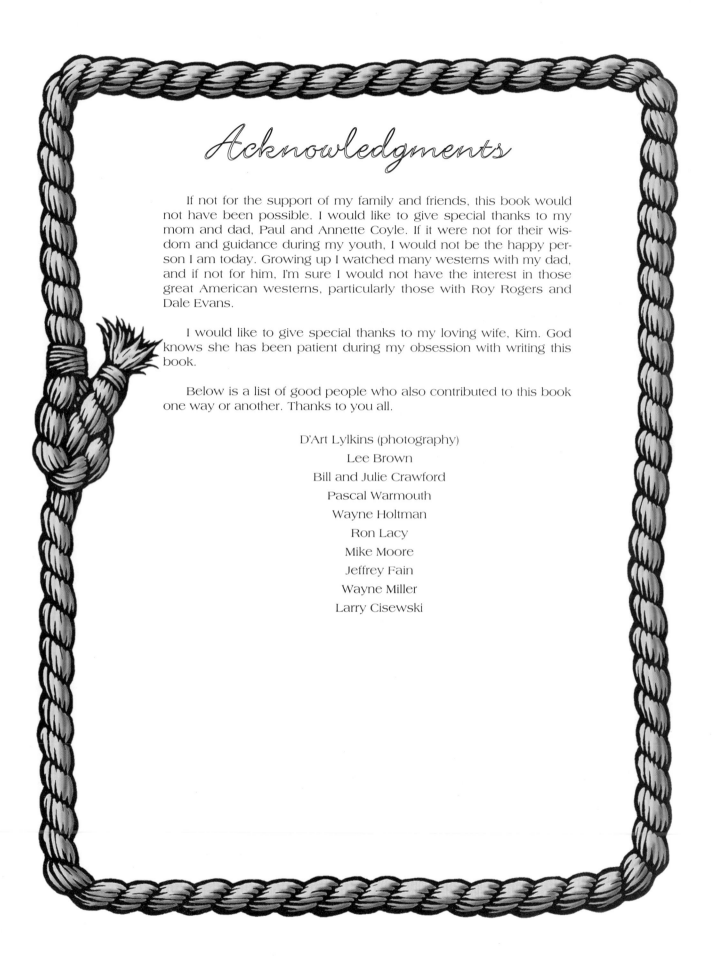

Acknowledgments

If not for the support of my family and friends, this book would not have been possible. I would like to give special thanks to my mom and dad, Paul and Annette Coyle. If it were not for their wisdom and guidance during my youth, I would not be the happy person I am today. Growing up I watched many westerns with my dad, and if not for him, I'm sure I would not have the interest in those great American westerns, particularly those with Roy Rogers and Dale Evans.

I would like to give special thanks to my loving wife, Kim. God knows she has been patient during my obsession with writing this book.

Below is a list of good people who also contributed to this book one way or another. Thanks to you all.

D'Art Lylkins (photography)
Lee Brown
Bill and Julie Crawford
Pascal Warmouth
Wayne Holtman
Ron Lacy
Mike Moore
Jeffrey Fain
Wayne Miller
Larry Cisewski

Foreword

Back in the 1940s and 1950s we baby boomers had it pretty good! The world was at peace and the nation's thoughts turned to happier things. Television was relatively new and, like most kids, my eyes were glued to the tiny screen watching westerns. At one time, western shows accounted for almost 75% of television programming. Along with these great shows came commercials, promoting everything from detergent to deodorant to my favorite—toys.

Every kid I knew wanted cowboy toys and, my favorite was Roy Rogers (wonder why?). Dad had his name on at least 450 different licensed items. For every licensed item, there were as many unlicensed. I don't know if anyone really knows how many items are out there.

When Allan Coyle asked me to do the foreword for this book, I was thrilled! Many times in the past folks have come to me asking to do a price guide on Roy Rogers and Dale Evans collectibles. This is the only one I know of in print. Allan has taken painstaking steps in finding and fairly pricing items in this guide.

I can't begin to tell you how many times I have been asked the value of a certain item. All I can tell you is it's worth whatever someone will give you for it! Sometimes you might have the one piece that a collector needs. Will he pay a little more for that item to complete his collection? You betcha!

I also enjoy collecting, and am very excited when I find something new or in mint-in-the-box condition. I've never outgrown my love for toys, especially Roy Rogers and Dale Evans toys!

Good luck collecting and Happy Trails Always!

Dusty Rogers

The author with Dusty Rogers.

Introduction

When baby boomers like myself hear the names Roy Rogers or Dale Evans, they immediately visualize the fabulous 40s, 50s, and early 60s. Due to their success in radio, movies, and television many manufacturers of toys, food, and other products wanted Roy's and Dale's endorsements, and thousands of Roy Rogers and Dale Evans items were produced during that grand era.

The baby boomers of the 40s and 50s are now in their 40s and 50s and yearn to possess a piece of their childhood to remind them of a much simpler time. By collecting these great old toys and collectibles you somehow feel like you have traveled back in time. During the mid to late 1990s, interest in memorabilia of the 50s increased greatly, forcing prices for excellent to mint pieces to go through the roof. The public was forced to begin searching their attics and basements, and items began to surface at antique shows like never before. And since the introduction of Internet auctions, even more items have begun to surface. Up to a couple of years ago even mediocre items like lunch boxes, scarves, and cereal premiums were bringing significant prices, but due to so-called "flooding the market," many items have seen a downward turn in value. Most excellent to mint condition items continue to hold their own.

Buying and Collecting as an Investment

When I began collecting Roy Rogers and Dale Evans items in the early 1990s, it was very difficult to find toys in excellent to mint condition. I very seldom saw any item in its original box or package and when I did the prices were so escalated, it made it nearly impossible to purchase them. Items rarely seen on the open market, that may have taken years to acquire by going to estate auctions and antique malls, were now obtainable due to the Internet at a much faster pace. As I mentioned earlier, most items have seen a downward turn in value due to the many items now available on the Internet. It is hard to say what the future holds as far as values. I would think that there will be even more people beginning to collect and supply and demand dictates prices. As an example, only so many original Roy Rogers and Dale Evans lunch boxes were produced in the 1950s and early 1960s. If the interest does increase, prices will more than likely soar again.

Identifying and Pricing

This book was assembled to be user-friendly for collectors as well as dealers. This is the first identification and value guide written solely for Roy Rogers and Dale Evans toys and memorabilia. There is no doubt many items are not listed here, but hopefully more items will be listed in the next version.

Prices are most often dictated by supply and demand. But please keep in mind just because an item may be scarce does not mean it will fetch a high dollar. If an item is scarce most often it will be in demand, but not always. As of the writing of this book, cap guns rank number one as far as bringing the highest prices due to demand. When you have an item that is scarce and in great demand you can expect the price to be marked too high for the average collector.

In this book I have adopted three well-known classifications.

C10 — Mint meaning never played with, in new, unused condition.

C8 — Very good, excellent meaning slightly played with, showing little wear or use.

C6 — Good, evidence of overall wear, has been played with but is still desirable to some collectors.

Box Reproduction Alert:

Due to escalating demand over the past few years and the desirability of original boxes, boxes have been reproduced and sold as originals. Personally, I don't have a problem with boxes being reproduced as long as they are marked as a reproduction, but most often they are not and due to the laser printers of today, it is nearly impossible to sort the new from the old with the naked eye. Under a strong magnifying glass original boxes will show a dot pattern and reproduced lasers will show a faint line pattern. When you compare the two it is easy to determine which is the original.

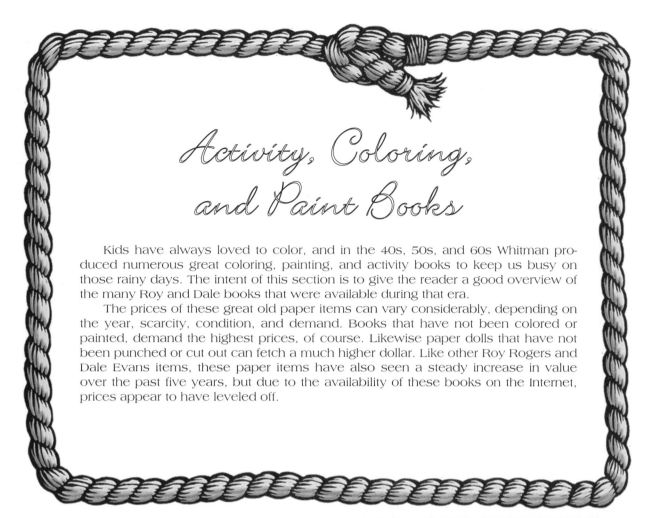

Activity, Coloring, and Paint Books

Kids have always loved to color, and in the 40s, 50s, and 60s Whitman produced numerous great coloring, painting, and activity books to keep us busy on those rainy days. The intent of this section is to give the reader a good overview of the many Roy and Dale books that were available during that era.

The prices of these great old paper items can vary considerably, depending on the year, scarcity, condition, and demand. Books that have not been colored or painted, demand the highest prices, of course. Likewise paper dolls that have not been punched or cut out can fetch a much higher dollar. Like other Roy Rogers and Dale Evans items, these paper items have also seen a steady increase in value over the past five years, but due to the availability of these books on the Internet, prices appear to have leveled off.

Roy Rogers Coloring Book, 8½" x 11", Whitman #1066, copyright 1946. C10–$65.00; C8–$35.00; C6–$15.00.

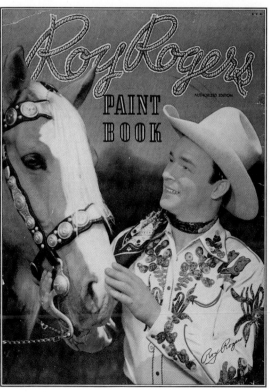

Roy Rogers Paint Book, 11" x 15", Whitman #1158, copyright 1948. C10–$50.00; C8–$25.00; C6–$15.00.

Roy Rogers and Dale Evans Paint Book, 11" x 15", Whitman #1120-15, copyright 1950. C10–$65.00; C8–$35.00; C6–$15.00.

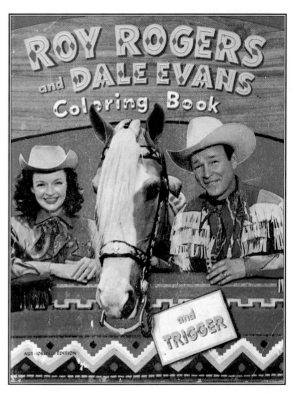

Roy Rogers and Dale Evans and Trigger Coloring Book, 8½" x 11", Whitman #217125, copyright 1951. C10–$50.00; C8–$25.00; C6–$15.00.

Roy Rogers and Dale Evans Coloring Book, 8½" x 11", Rohr Co. #1116-15, copyright 1951. C10–$55.00; C8–$30.00; C6–$15.00.

Roy Rogers and Dale Evans Coloring Book, 8½" x 11", Whitman #214625, copyright 1952. C10–$60.00; C8–$35.00; C6–$20.00.

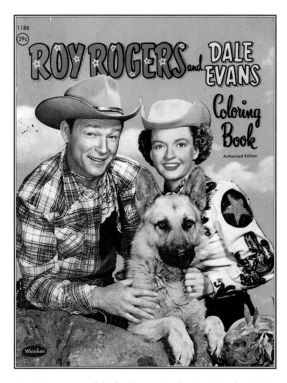

Roy Rogers and Dale Evans Coloring Book, 8½" x 11", Whitman #1186, copyright 1953. C10–$50.00; C8–$25.00; C6–$15.00.

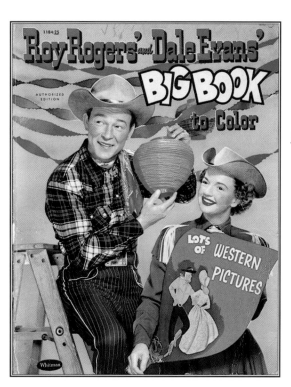

Roy Rogers' and Dale Evans' Big Book to Color, 8½" x 11", Whitman #1184:25, copyright 1954. C10–$50.00; C8–$25.00; C6–$15.00.

Roy Rogers and Dale Evans Coloring Book, 8½" x 11", Whitman #1184, copyright 1955. C10–$55.00; C8–$30.00; C6–$20.00.

Roy Rogers' Double-R-Bar Ranch Coloring and Many Things to Do Book, 8½" x 11", Whitman #1035-49, copyright 1955. C10–$60.00; C8–$35.00; C6–$20.00.

Roy Rogers and Dale Evans Double-R-Bar Ranch Coloring Book, 8½" x 11", Whitman #1035:49, copyright 1956. C10–$50.00; C8–$30.00; C6–$15.00.

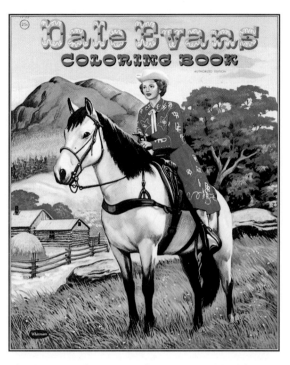

Dale Evans Coloring Book, 11½" x 13", Whitman #1755, copyright 1957. C10–$50.00; C8–$25.00; C6–$15.00.

Roy Rogers and Dale Evans Coloring Book, 8½" x 11", Whitman #2946, copyright 1959. C10–$40.00; C8–$20.00; C6–$10.00.

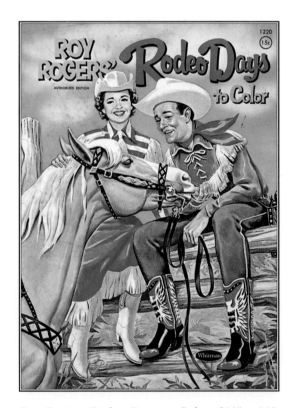

Roy Rogers Rodeo Days to Color, 8½" x 11", Whitman #1220, copyright 1962. C10–$40.00; C8–$20.00; C6–$10.00.

Roy Rogers' Pal Pat Brady Coloring Book, 8½"
x 11", Whitman #1255, copyright 1955.
C10–$40.00; C8–$25.00; C6 –$10.00.

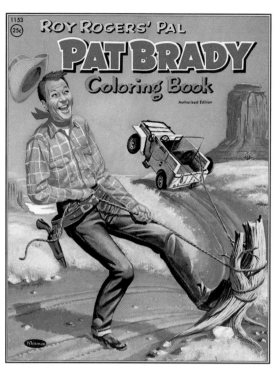

Roy Rogers' Pal Pat Brady Coloring Book, 8½" x
11", Whitman #1153, copyright 1956.
C10–$40.00; C8–$25.00; C6–$10.00.

Roy Rogers' Trigger & Bullet Coloring Book,
8½" x 11", Whitman #2958, copyright 1956.
C10–$35.00; C8–$20.00; C6–$10.00.

Roy Rogers' Trigger & Bullet Coloring Book,
6½" x 7½", Whitman #1315, copyright 1959.
C10–$30.00; C8–$15.00; C6–$5.00.

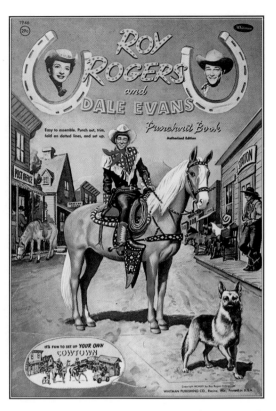

Roy Rogers' Annual, 8½" x 11", Whitman #4058:49, copyright 1954. C10–$50.00; C8–$30.00; C6–$20.00.

Roy Rogers and Dale Evans Punch-Out Book, 11" x 15", Whitman #1949, copyright 1952. C10–$100.00; C8–$50.00; C6–$25.00.

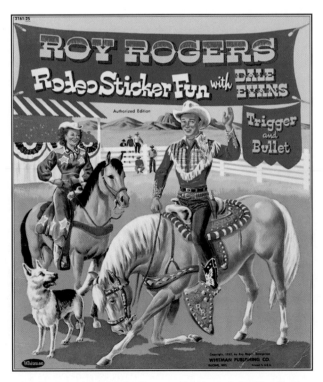

Roy Rogers with Dale Evans, Trigger & Bullet Rodeo Sticker Fun Book, 10½" x 12", Whitman #2161, copyright 1953. C10–$75.00; C8–$40.00; C6–$20.00.

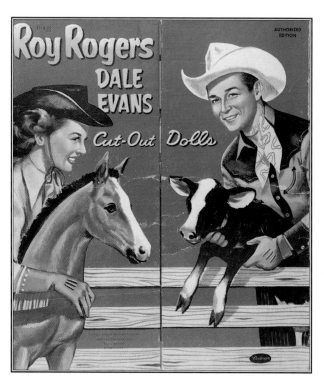

Roy Rogers Dale Evans Cut-Out Dolls, 10½" x 12", Whitman #1184:25, copyright 1954. C10–$80.00; C8–$45.00; C6–$25.00.

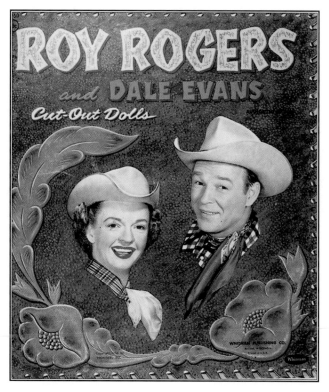

Roy Rogers and Dale Evans Cut-Out Dolls, 10½" x 12", Whitman #1950, copyright 1954. C10–$90.00; C8–$50.00; C6–$25.00.

Comic Books and Related Items

In the 40s, 50s, and early 60s millions of kids would go to their local drug store or market and buy their new issue of Roy Rogers or Dale Evans comic books for a whopping 10 cents. Each month there would be a front cover color photo of Roy either riding Trigger, fighting the bad guy, or holding an arm load of puppies, usually with Roy displaying his million-dollar smile. These comics were full-color adventures of Roy, Trigger, and Bullet.

The Roy Rogers comic book legacy began in April of 1944 when the Four-Color Series began. Then Dell comics began with #1 Roy Rogers comic in January 1948 which ended in September – October 1961 with #145. Not to be outdone Trigger and Dale Evans would also have their own comic series in the 50s.

Scarcity and condition are the most important things to remember when purchasing or selling your comic books.

Note: These comic covers are available in color on cards from Arrow Catch Productions for $19.95 plus $4.50 for shipping. Call or write Arrow Catch Productions, 1029 Vernon Way, El Cajon, CA 92020. 619-562-9962.

Four-Color Comic Books

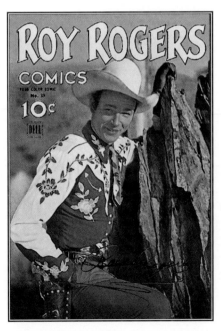

#38, April 1944. C10–$750.00; C8–$400.00; C6–$100.00.

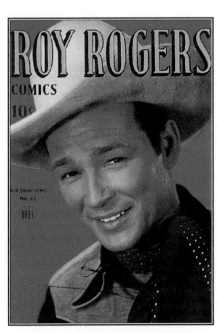

#63, January 1945. C10–$350.00; C8–$150.00; C6–$35.00.

#86, October 1945. C10–$250.00;
C8–$125.00; C6–$25.00.

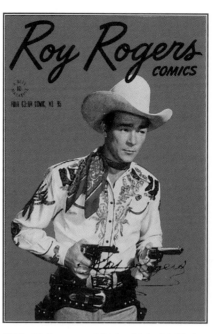

#95, February 1946. C10–$250.00;
C8–$125.00; C6–$25.00.

#109, June 1946. C10–$175.00;
C8–$75.00; C6–$25.00.

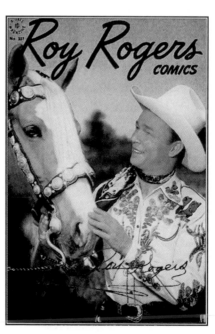

#117, September 1946. C10–$125.00;
C8–$50.00; C6–$20.00.

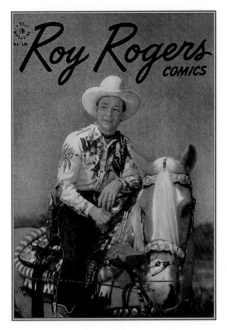

#124, November 1946. C10–$125.00;
C8–$50.00; C6–$20.00.

#137, February 1947. C10–$125.00;
C8–$50.00; C6–$20.00.

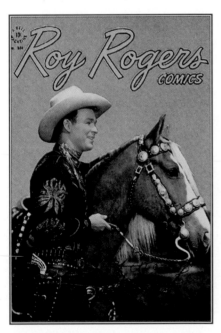

#144, April 1947. C10–$125.00;
C8–$50.00; C6–$20.00.

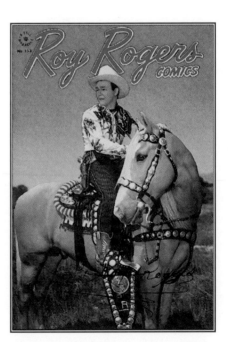

#153, June 1947. C10–$75.00;
C8–$35.00; C6–$15.00.

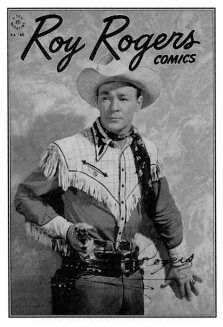

#160, August 1947. C10–$95.00;
C8–$45.00; C6–$15.00.

#166, October 1947. C10–$95.00;
C8–$45.00; C6–$15.00.

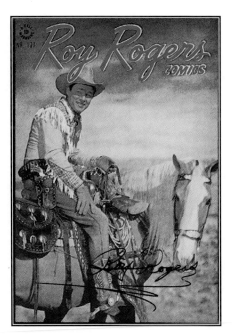

#177, December 1947. C10–$95.00;
C8–$45.00; C6–$15.00.

#1, January 1948. C10–$350.00;
C8–$150.00; C6–$50.00.

#2, February 1948. C10–$155.00;
C8–$75.00; C6–$25.00.

#3, March 1948. C10–$125.00;
C8–$55.00; C6–$20.00.

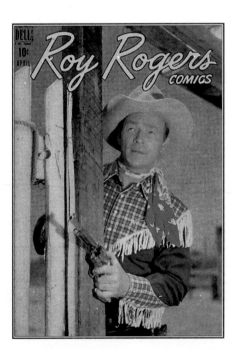

#4, April 1948. C10–$125.00;
C8–$55.00; C6–$20.00.

#5, May 1948. C10–$125.00; C8–$55.00; C6–$20.00.

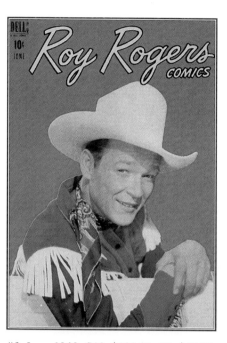

#6, June 1948. C10–$100.00; C8–$45.00; C6–$15.00.

#7, July 1948. C10–$100.00; C8–$45.00; C6–$15.00.

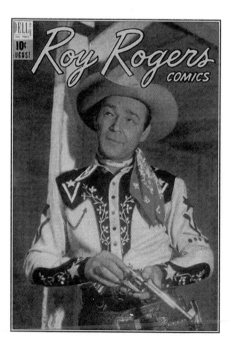

#8, August 1948. C10–$90.00; C8–$40.00; C6–$15.00.

#9, September 1948. C10–$90.00; C8–$40.00; C6–$15.00.

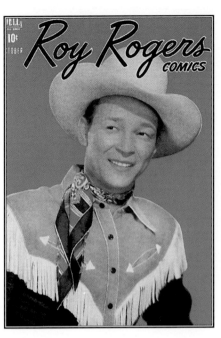

#10, October 1948. C10–$90.00; C8–$40.00; C6–$15.00.

#11, November 1948. C10–$85.00; C8–$35.00; C6–$12.00.

#12, December 1948. C10–$65.00; C8–$30.00; C6–$10.00.

#13, January 1949. C10–$65.00; C8–$30.00; C6–$10.00.

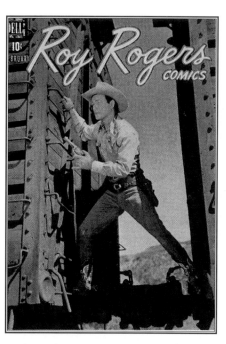

#14, February 1949. C10–$65.00; C8–$30.00; C6–$10.00.

#15, March 1949. C10–$65.00; C8–$30.00; C6–$10.00.

#16, April 1949. C10–$65.00; C8–$30.00; C6–$10.00.

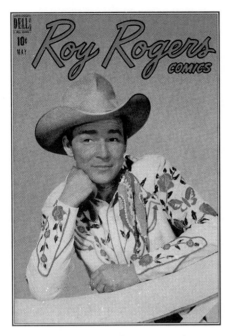

#17, May 1949. C10–$65.00; C8–$30.00; C6–$10.00.

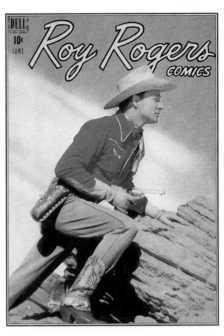

#18, June 1949. C10–$65.00; C8–$30.00; C6–$10.00.

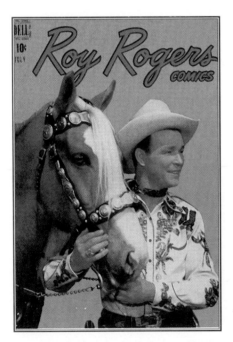

#19, July 1949. C10–$65.00; C8–$30.00; C6–$10.00.

#20, August 1949. C10–$55.00; C8–$25.00; C6–$8.00.

#21, September 1949. C10–$55.00;
C8–$25.00; C6–$8.00.

#22, October 1949. C10–$55.00;
C8–$25.00; C6–$8.00.

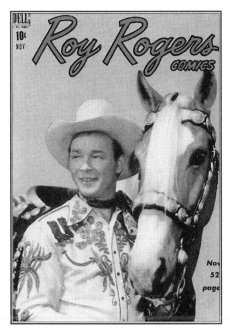

#23, November 1949. C10–$55.00;
C8–$25.00; C6–$8.00.

#24, December 1949. C10–$55.00;
C8–$25.00; C6–$8.00.

#25, January 1950. C10–$55.00;
C8–$25.00; C6–$8.00.

#26, February 1950. C10–$55.00;
C8–$25.00; C6–$8.00.

#27, March 1950. C10–$55.00; C8–$25.00;
C6–$8.00.

#28, April 1950. C10–$55.00; C8–$25.00;
C6–$8.00.

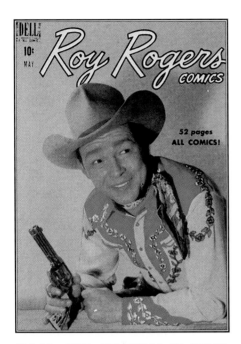

#29, May 1950. C10–$55.00; C8–$25.00;
C6–$8.00.

#30, June 1950. C10–$55.00; C8–$25.00;
C6–$8.00.

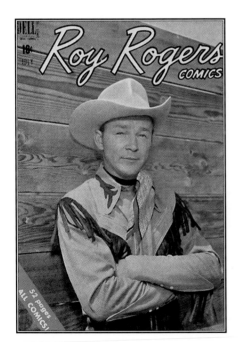

#31, July 1950. C10–$45.00; C8–$20.00;
C6–$7.00.

#32, August 1950. C10–$45.00; C8–$20.00;
C6–$7.00.

#33, September 1950. C10–$45.00;
C8–$20.00; C6–$7.00.

#34, October 1950. C10–$45.00;
C8–$20.00; C6–$7.00.

#35, November 1950. C10–$45.00;
C8–$20.00; C6–$7.00.

#36, December 1950. C10–$45.00;
C8–$20.00; C6–$7.00.

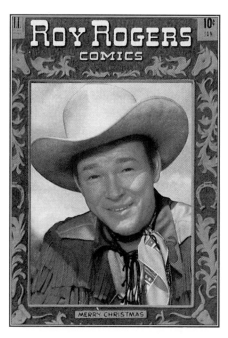

#37, January 1951. C10–$45.00; C8–$20.00; C6–$7.00.

#38, February 1951. C10–$45.00; C8–$20.00; C6–$7.00.

#39, March 1951. C10–$45.00; C8–$20.00; C6–$7.00.

#40, April 1951. C10–$45.00; C8–$20.00; C6–$7.00.

#41, May 1951. C10–$45.00; C8–$20.00; C6–$7.00.

#42, June 1951. C10–$45.00; C8–$20.00; C6–$7.00.

#43, July 1951. C10–$45.00; C8–$20.00; C6–$7.00.

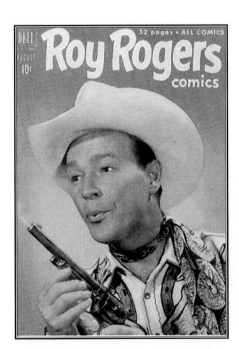

#44, August 1951. C10–$45.00; C8–$20.00; C6–$7.00.

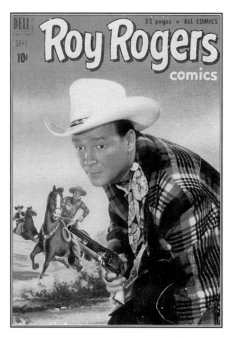

#45, September 1951. C10–$45.00;
C8–$20.00; C6–$7.00.

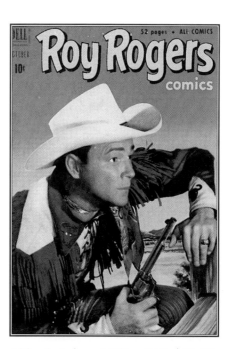

#46, October 1951. C10–$45.00;
C8–$20.00; C6–$7.00.

#47, November 1951. C10–$30.00;
C8–$15.00; C6–$5.00.

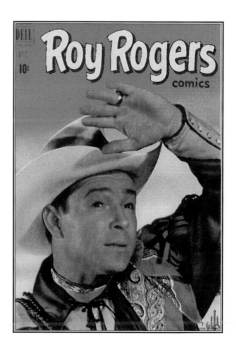

#48, December 1951. C10–$30.00;
C8–$15.00; C6–$5.00.

#49, January 1952. C10–$30.00;
C8–$15.00; C6–$5.00.

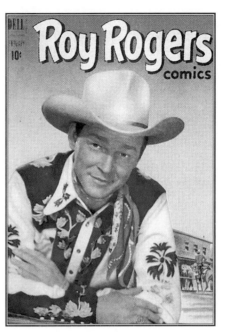

#50, February 1952. C10–$30.00;
C8–$15.00; C6–$5.00.

#51, March 1952. C10–$30.00;
C8–$15.00; C6–$5.00.

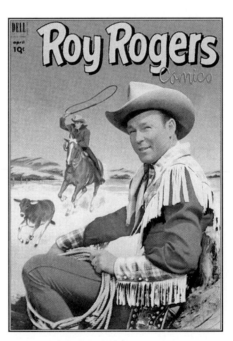

#52, April 1952. C10–$30.00;
C8–$15.00; C6–$5.00.

#53, May 1952. C10–$30.00; C8–$15.00;
C6–$5.00.

#54, June 1952. C10–$30.00; C8–$15.00;
C6–$5.00.

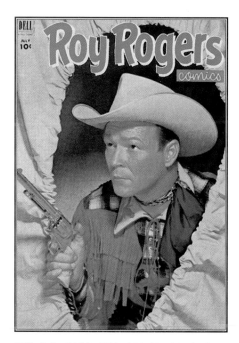

#55, July 1952. C10–$30.00; C8–$15.00;
C6–$5.00.

#56, August 1952. C10–$30.00;
C8–$15.00; C6–$5.00.

#57, September 1952. C10–$35.00;
C8–$18.00; C6–$6.00.

#58, October 1952. C10–$25.00;
C8–$12.00; C6–$5.00.

#59, November 1952. C10–$25.00;
C8–$12.00; C6–$5.00.

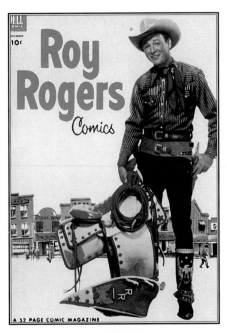

#60, December 1952. C10–$25.00;
C8–$12.00; C6–$5.00.

#61, January 1953. C10–$25.00;
C8–$12.00; C6–$5.00.

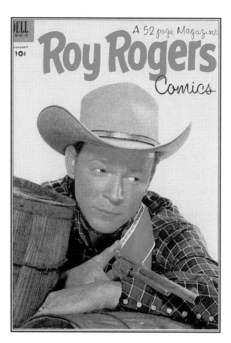

#62, February 1953. C10–$25.00;
C8–$12.00; C6–$5.00.

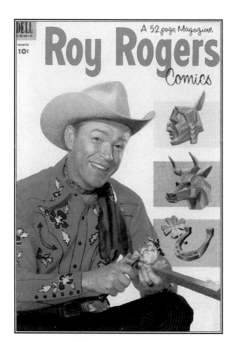

#63, March 1953. C10–$25.00; C8–$12.00;
C6–$5.00.

#64, April 1953. C10–$25.00; C8–$12.00;
C6–$5.00.

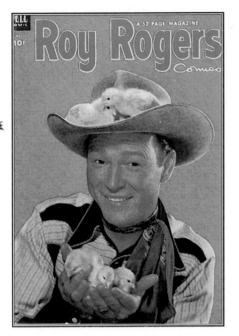

#65, May 1953. C10–$25.00; C8–$12.00; C6–$5.00.

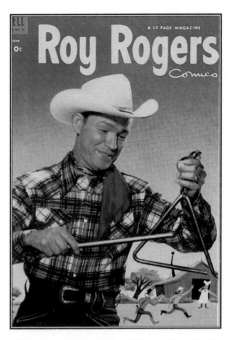

#66, June 1953. C10–$25.00; C8–$12.00; C6–$5.00.

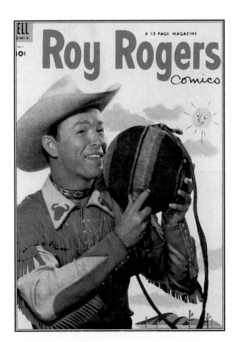

#67, July 1953. C10–$25.00; C8–$12.00; C6–$5.00.

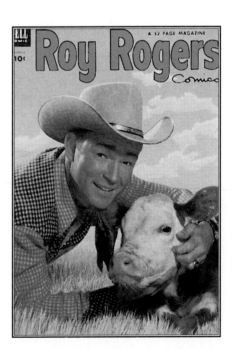

#68, August 1953. C10–$25.00; C8–$12.00; C6–$5.00.

#69, September 1953. C10–$25.00;
C8–$12.00; C6–$5.00.

#70, October 1953. C10–$25.00;
C8–$12.00; C6–$5.00.

#71, November 1953. C10–$23.00;
C8–$11.00; C6–$4.50.

#72, December 1953. C10–$23.00;
C8–$11.00; C6–$4.50.

#73, January 1954. C10–$23.00; C8–$11.00; C6–$4.50.

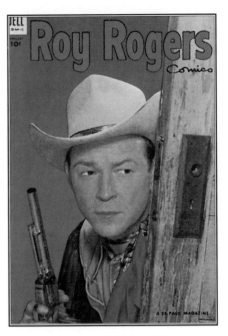

#74, February 1954. C10–$23.00; C8–$11.00; C6–$4.50.

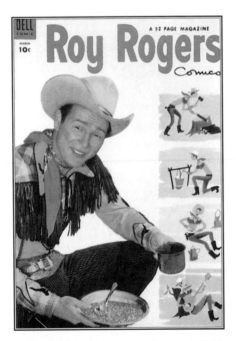

#75, March 1954. C10–$23.00; C8–$11.00; C6–$4.50.

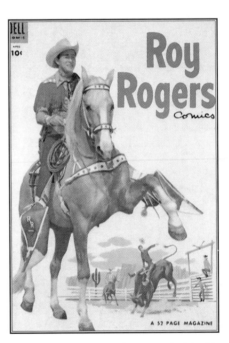

#76, April 1954. C10–$23.00; C8–$11.00; C6–$4.50.

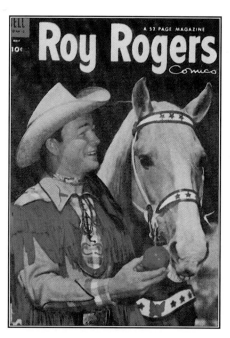

#77, May 1954. C10–$23.00; C8–$11.00; C6–$4.50.

#78, June 1954. C10–$23.00; C8–$11.00; C6–$4.50.

#79, July 1954. C10–$23.00; C8–$11.00; C6–$4.50.

#80, August 1954. C10–$23.00; C8–$11.00; C6–$4.50.

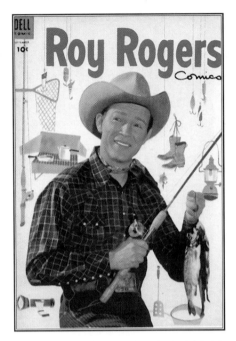

#81, September 1954. C10–$20.00;
C8–$10.00; C6–$4.00.

#82, October 1954. C10–$20.00;
C8–$10.00; C6–$4.00.

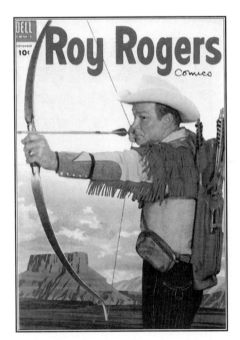

#83, November 1954. C10–$20.00;
C8–$10.00; C6–$4.00.

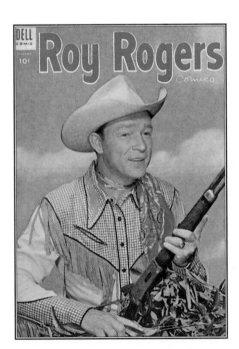

#84, December 1954. C10–$20.00;
C8–$10.00; C6–$4.00.

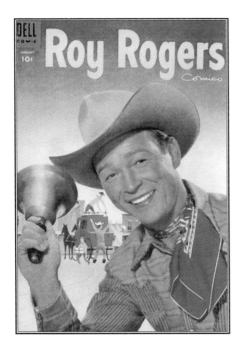

#85, January 1955. C10–$20.00;
C8–$10.00; C6–$4.00.

#86, February 1955. C10–$20.00;
C8–$10.00; C6–$4.00.

#87, March 1955. C10–$20.00;
C8–$10.00; C6–$4.00.

#88, April 1955. C10–$20.00;
C8–$10.00; C6–$4.00.

#89, May 1955. C10–$20.00; C8–$10.00; C6–$4.00.

#90, June 1955. C10–$20.00; C8–$10.00; C6–$4.00.

#91, July 1955. C10–$20.00; C8–$10.00; C6–$4.00.

#92, August 1955. C10–$20.00; C8–$10.00; C6–$4.00.

#93, September 1955. C10–$20.00;
C8–$10.00; C6–$4.00.

#94, October 1955. C10–$20.00;
C8–$10.00; C6–$4.00.

#95, November 1955. C10–$20.00;
C8–$10.00; C6–$4.00.

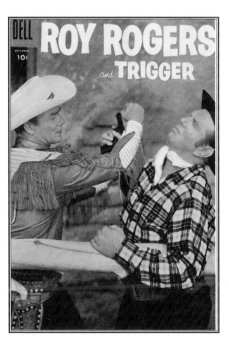

#96, December 1955. C10–$20.00;
C8–$10.00; C6–$4.00.

#97, January 1956. C10–$20.00; C8–$10.00; C6–$4.00.

#98, February 1956. C10–$20.00; C8–$10.00; C6–$4.00.

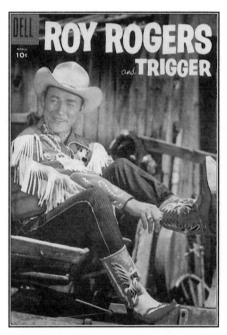

#99, March 1956. C10–$20.00; C8–$10.00; C6–$4.00.

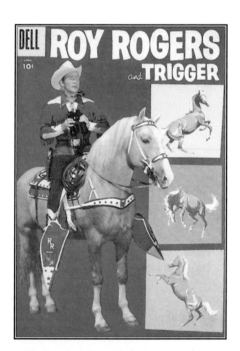

#100, April 1956. C10–$30.00; C8–$15.00; C6–$5.00.

#101, May 1956. C10–$20.00; C8–$10.00; C6–$4.00.

#102, June 1956. C10–$20.00; C8–$10.00; C6–$4.00.

#103, July 1956. C10–$20.00; C8–$10.00; C6–$4.00.

#104, August 1956. C10–$20.00; C8–$10.00; C6–$4.00.

#105, September 1956. C10–$20.00; C8–$10.00; C6–$4.00.

#106, October 1956. C10–$20.00; C8–$10.00; C6–$4.00.

#107, November 1956. C10–$20.00; C8–$10.00; C6–$4.00.

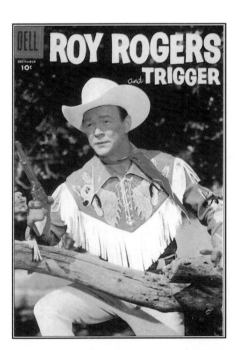

#108, December 1956. C10–$20.00; C8–$10.00; C6–$4.00.

#109, January 1957. C10–$20.00;
C8–$10.00; C6–$4.00.

#110, February 1957. C10–$20.00;
C8–$10.00; C6–$4.00.

#111, March 1957. C10–$35.00;
C8–$18.00; C6–$7.00.

#112, April 1957. C10–$20.00;
C8–$10.00; C6–$4.00.

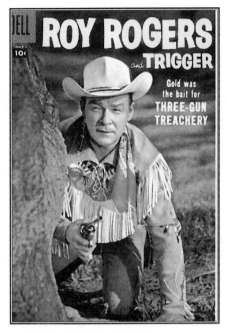

#113, May 1957. C10–$20.00; C8–$10.00; C6–$4.00.

#114, June 1957. C10–$20.00; C8–$10.00; C6–$4.00.

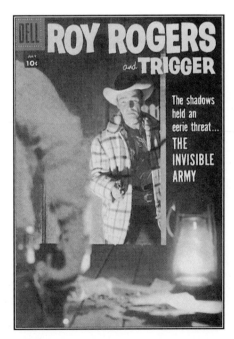

#115, July 1957. C10–$20.00; C8–$10.00; C6–$4.00.

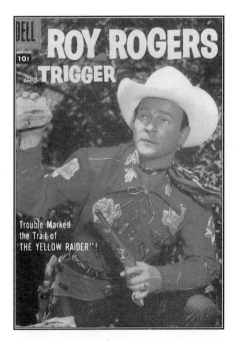

#116, August 1957. C10–$20.00; C8–$10.00; C6–$4.00.

#117, September 1957. C10–$20.00; C8–$10.00; C6–$4.00.

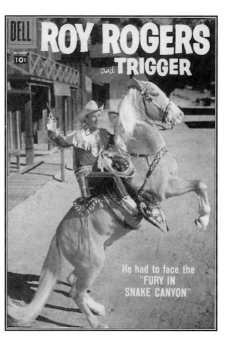

#118, October 1957. C10–$20.00; C8–$10.00; C6–$4.00.

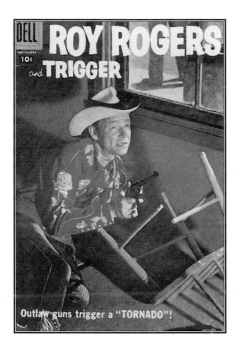

#119, November 1957. C10–$35.00; C8–$18.00; C6–$7.00.

#120, December 1957. C10–$35.00; C8–$18.00; C6–$7.00.

#121, January 1958. C10–$35.00;
C8–$18.00; C6–$7.00.

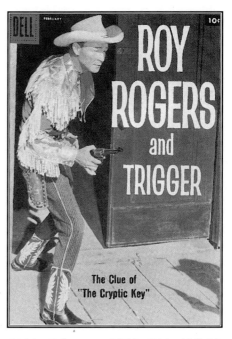

#122, February 1958. C10–$35.00;
C8–$18.00; C6–$7.00.

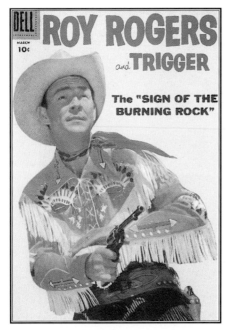

#123, March 1958. C10–$35.00;
C8–$18.00; C6–$7.00.

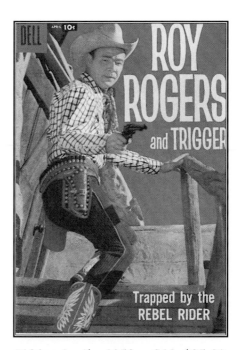

#124, April 1958. C10–$35.00;
C8–$18.00; C6–$7.00.

#125, May 1958. C10–$23.00; C8–$11.00; C6–$4.50.

#126, July-August 1958. C10–$23.00; C8–$11.00; C6–$4.50.

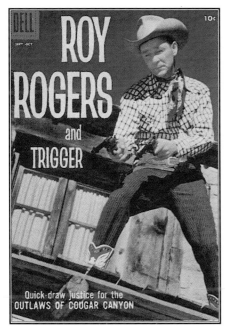

#127, September-October 1958. C10–$23.00; C8–$11.00; C6–$4.50.

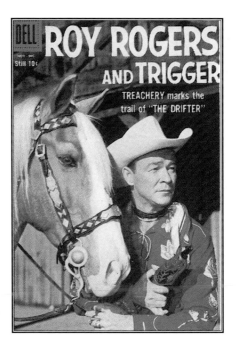

#128, November-December 1958. C10–$23.00; C8–$11.00; C6–$4.50.

#129, January-February 1959. C10–$23.00; C8–$11.00; C6–$4.50.

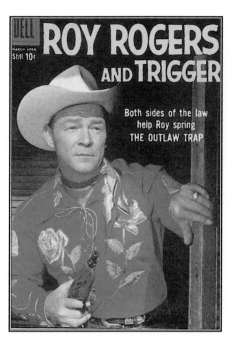

#130, March-April 1959. C10–$23.00; C8–$11.00; C6–$4.50.

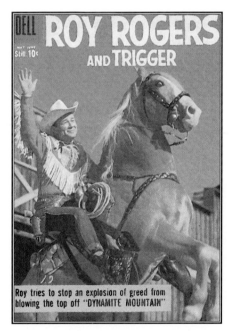

#131, May-June 1959. C10–$23.00; C8–$11.00; C6–$4.50.

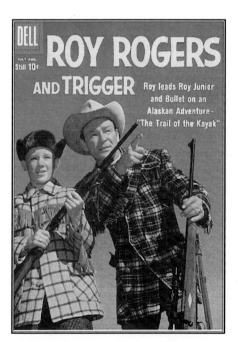

#132, July-August 1959. C10–$25.00; C8–$12.00; C6–$5.00.

#133,   September-October   1959.
C10–$25.00; C8–$12.00; C6–$5.00.

#134, November-December 1959.
C10–$25.00; C8–$12.00; C6–$5.00.

#135,   January-February   1960.
C10–$25.00; C8–$12.00; C6–$5.00.

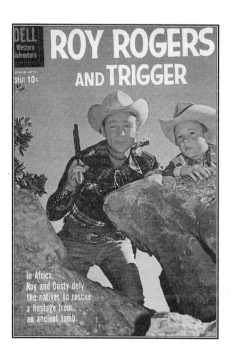

#136, March-April 1960. C10–$25.00;
C8–$12.00; C6–$5.00.

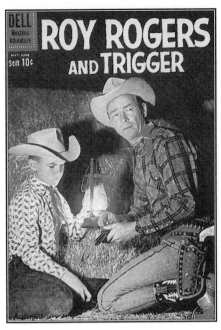

#137, May-June 1960. C10–$25.00;
C8–$12.00; C6–$5.00.

#138, July-August 1960. C10–$25.00;
C8–$12.00; C6–$5.00.

#139, September-October 1960.
C10–$25.00; C8–$12.00; C6–$5.00.

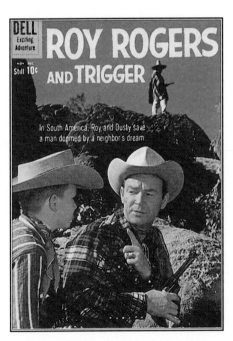

#140, November-December 1960.
C10–$25.00; C8–$12.00; C6–$5.00.

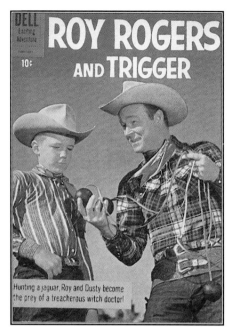

#141, January-February 1961. C10–$25.00; C8–$12.00; C6–$5.00.

#142, March-April 1961. C10–$25.00; C8–$12.00; C6–$5.00.

#143, May-June 1961. C10–$25.00; C8–$12.00; C6–$5.00.

#144, July-August 1961. C10–$25.00; C8–$12.00; C6–$5.00.

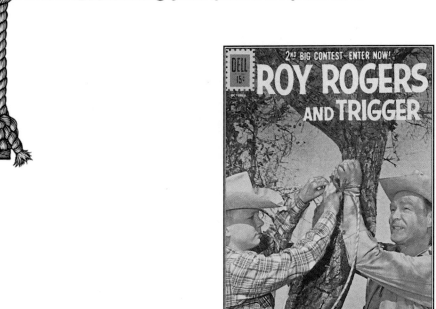

#145, September-October 1961.
C10–$35.00; C8–$18.00; C6–$6.00.

Miscellaneous Comics, Magazines, and Related Items

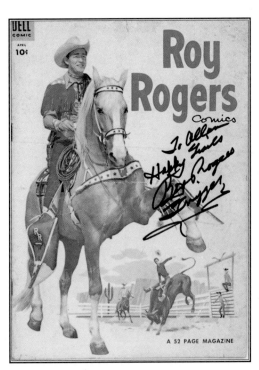

Roy Rogers personally autographed comic #76, April 1954, "To Allan Happy Trails Roy Rogers & Trigger." $150.00.

Roy Rogers personally autographed comic #109, January 1957, "To Allan Best Wishes Roy Rogers & Trigger." $150.00.

March of Comics 1955, store giveaway, back cover reads
"Keystone Shoes." C10–$65.00; C8–$40.00; C6–$20.00.

Roy Rogers — Series 1 Premium Collector Card Set includes issue #1 January 1948 through #70 October 1953. Series 2 Collector Card Set includes #71 November 1953 through October 1961 plus 13 Roy Rogers four-color comics beginning April 1944 through December 1947.

57

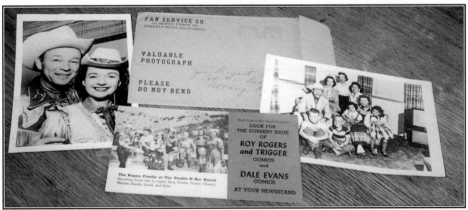

Roy Rogers and Dale Evans Dell Comics mailer, includes two 5" x 6" black and white photos and Dell Comics postcard and original envelope. Complete $75.00.

Roy Rogers original newspaper comic art, 23" x 8½", white art sheet in black ink, by Arens, August 14, 1950, fine print reads "CORP. 1950 King Features Syndicate, Inc. World Rights Reserved." $150.00 – 200.00.

Roy Rogers original newspaper comic art, 5½" x 17½", white art sheet in black ink, by Arens, July 18, 1959. $100.00 – 150.00.

Roy Rogers original Sunday newspaper comic art, 27" x 19", white art sheet in black, by Al McKimson, September 24, 1961, signed "To John Happy Trails Roy Rogers & Trigger." $500.00 – 750.00.

Roy Rogers comic clippings from Sunday paper. $5.00 – 10.00 each.

Front cover of *Liberty* magazine, December 14, 1946.
C10–$50.00; C8–$35.00; C6–$15.00.

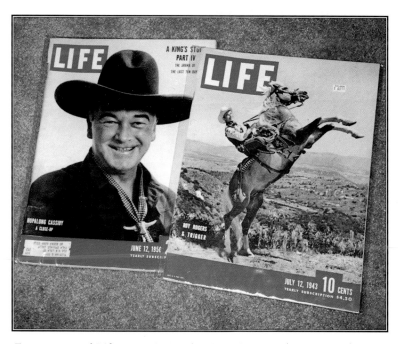

Front cover of *Life* magazine, July 12, 1943. C10–$75.00; C8–$50.00;
C6–$25.00.

Inspirational and Biographical Books

Roy Rogers and Dale Evans will always be known as "The King of the Cowboys" and "Queen of the West." Both have also been known throughout the United States and around the world for their strong Christian and spiritual beliefs. Dale has written numerous spiritual and biographical books, stemming primarily from the tragic loss of their only biological child, Robin, who was born with Downs Syndrome. Due to physical complications Robin lived only for a couple of years. Other books in this chapter include those about adopted daughter Debbie and son Sandy who both died tragically as well. Unfortunately Roy and Dale have not always had "Happy Trails." As Dale once said "if it were not for the storms you would not appreciate the sunshine." Roy and Dale both publicly acknowledged that their faith in God had pulled them through the sad times. Their biographies tell of how Len Slye from Duck Run, Ohio, made his way to California to become the "King of the Cowboys" and how Dale Evans (Francis Smith), a Texan by birth, went from a radio singer and entertainer to become "The Queen of the West." Dusty Rogers's book reminisces about how he and his brother and sisters survived being kids of the famous western stars.

These types of books generally will range in price from $5 to $35, depending on the content and author. Many books authored by Dale Evans have been reissued in paperback form which usually will sell at a lower price than the original hardbacks. Biographies with photos are more desirable and will fetch a little higher price.

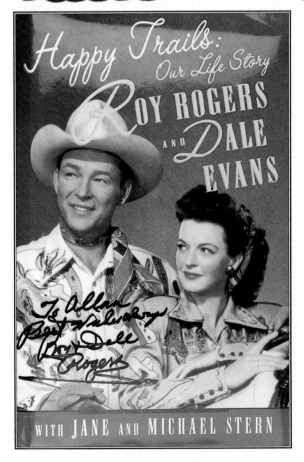

Happy Trails: Our Life Story, Roy Rogers and Dale Evans, 6½" x 9½", with Jane and Michael Stern, copyright 1994, signed "To Allan Best Wishes Always Roy Rogers & Dale." C10–$45.00; C8–$20.00; add $100.00 for autograph.

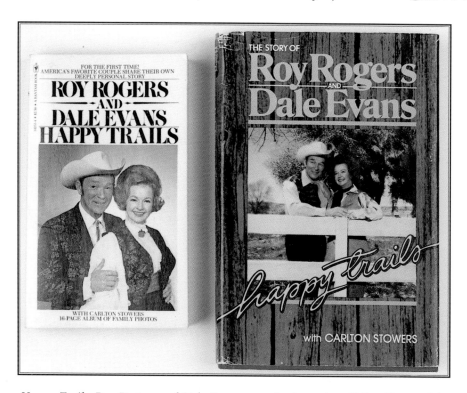

Happy Trails, Roy Rogers and Dale Evans paperback version, 6¾" x 4", copyright 1980. C10–$10.00.

The Story of Roy Rogers and Dale Evans "Happy Trails," with Carlton Stowers, 8½" x 6", Guidepost hardback version, copyright 1979. C10–$20.00; C8–$10.00; C6–$5.00.

Dearest Debbie (In Ai Lee) by Dale Evans Rogers, 5½" x 8", published Fleming H. Revell Company, copyright 1965. C10–$20.00; C8–$10.00; C6–$5.00.

Angel Unaware by Dale Evans Rogers, 5" x 7½", published by Fleming H. Revell Company, copyright 1958. C10–$25.00; C8–$12.00; C6–$5.00.

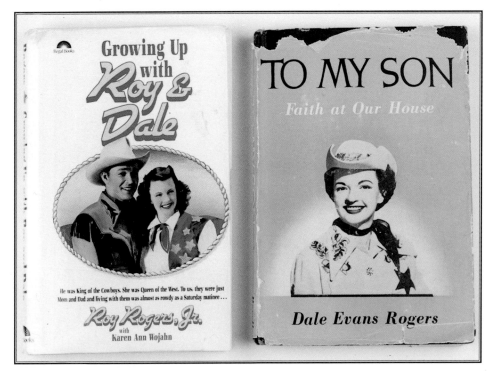

Growing Up with Roy and Dale, by Roy Rogers Jr., 9" x 6", by Regal Books, copyright 1973, 1978, and 1984. C10–$30.00; C8–$20.00; C6–$10.00.
To My Son: Faith at Our House by Dale Evans Rogers, 6" x 8½", Fleming H. Revel Co., copyright 1957. C10–$25.00; C8–$15.00; C6–$5.00.

Salute to Sandy by Dale Evans Rogers, 5½" x 8", published by Fleming H. Revel Co., copyright 1967. C10–$25.00; C8–$12.00; C6–$6.00.

Angel Unaware paperback version. C10–$10.00.

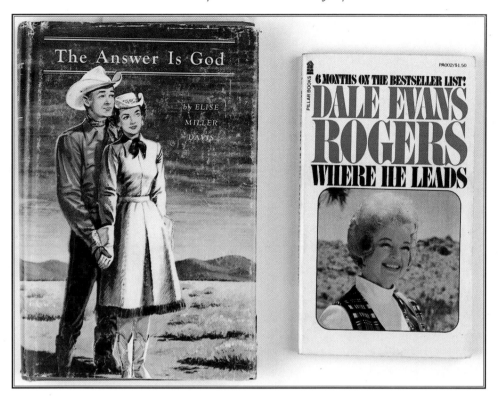

The Answer Is God by Elise Miller Davis, 8½" x 6", publisher McGraw-Hill Book Co., copyright 1955. C10–$35.00; C8–$20.00; C6–$10.00.

Where He Leads, Dale Evans Rogers, paperback version, publisher Pillar Books, copyright 1971. C10–$10.00.

Roy Rogers: King of the Cowboys, Collins Publishers, copyright 1994. C10–$35.00.

Prayer Book for Children, Dale Evans, 8½" x 11", Golden Press, copyright 1956. C10–$30.00; C8–$15.00; C6–$5.00.

Only One Star by Dale Evans Rogers, Word Publishing, copyright 1988. C10–$35.00.
In the Hands of the Potter by Dale Evans Rogers, Thomas Nelson Publishing, copyright 1994. C10–$35.00.
Trials, Tears and Triumph by Dale Evans Rogers, Fleming J. Revell, copyright 1977. C10–$25.00.

Let Us Love by Dale Evans Rogers, Words Books, copyright 1982. C10–$25.00.
Our Values by Dale Evans Rogers, Fleming H. Revell Co., copyright 1997. C10–$25.00.
Time Out, Ladies! by Dale Evans Rogers, Fleming H. Co., copyright 1966. C10–$20.00.

Dale: My Personal Picture Album by Dale
Evans Rogers, Fleming H. Revell, copyright
1971. C10–$25.00.

No Two Ways About It by Dale Evans Rogers, Fleming H. Revell Co., copyright 1963. C10–$25.00;
C8–$15.00; C6–$5.00.
My Spiritual Diary by Dale Evans Rogers, Fleming H. Revell Co., copyright 1955. C10–$25.00;
C8–$15.00; C6–$5.00.
Christmas is Always by Dale Evans Rogers. C10–$25.00.

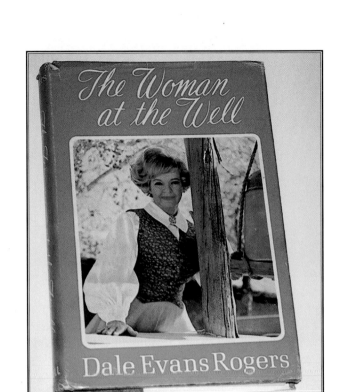

The Woman at the Well, Fleming H. Revell Publishing, copyright 1970. C10–$25.00.

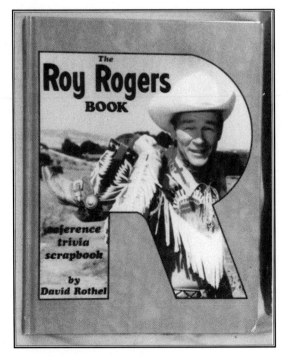

The Roy Rogers Book by David Rothel, Empire Publishing Inc., copyright 1987. C10–$35.00.

Story Books

    Back before The Cartoon Channel, Nickelodeon, The Disney Channel, and cable television in general, kids, as well as adults, could take a trip and never leave the farm by reading one of the many Roy Rogers and/or Dale Evans adventure books. There were several publishers who printed these great old books in the 40s, 50s, and early 60s. Many of these, such as The Little Golden Books, were written and illustrated for younger fans, but there were also several geared for young adults.

    The prices for these books can vary, depending on the year, condition, and demand. Books that have no tears or have their original book sleeves will usually fetch a higher price. Due to the availability of these books on the Internet, prices seem to have leveled off.

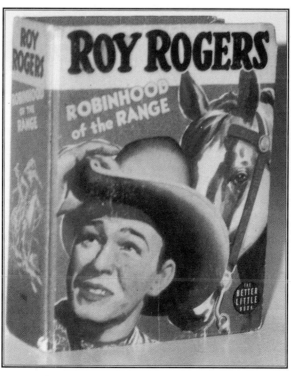

Roy Rogers: Robinhood on the Range, 3½" x 4½", Whitman Publishing Co., copyright 1942. C10–$65.00;C8–$35.00; C6–$15.00.

Roy Rogers and the Mystery of Howling Mesa, 3½" x 4½", Whitman Publishing Co., copyright 1948. C10–$65.00; C8–$35.00; C6–$15.00.

Roy Rogers: Range Detective, 5½" x 3", New Better Little Book, copyright 1949. C10–$50.00; C8–$30.00; C6–$15.00.

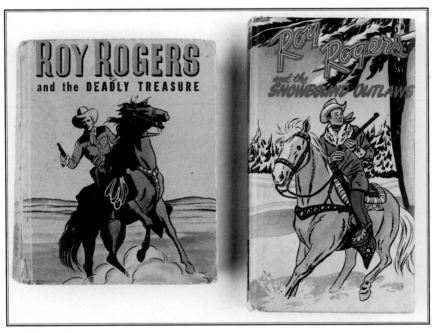

Roy Rogers and the Deadly Treasure, 4" x 4", Better Little Book, copyright 1947. C10–$65.00; C8–$40.00; C6–$15.00.
Roy Rogers and the Snowbound Outlaws, 5½" x 3", New Better Little Book, copyright 1948. C10–$50.00; C8–$30.00; C6–$15.00.

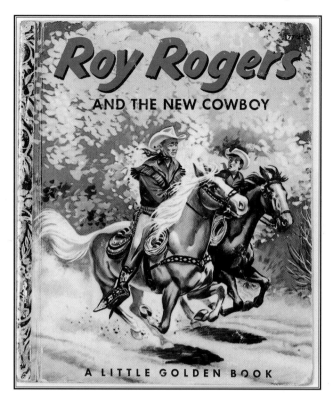

Roy Rogers and the New Cowboy, 6¾" x 8", Little Golden Book, copyright 1953. C10–$40.00; C8–$25.00; C6–$10.00.

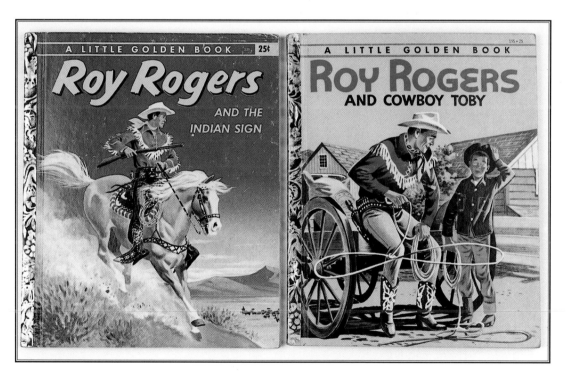

Roy Rogers and the Indian Sign, 6⅞" x 8", Little Golden Book, copyright 1956. C10–$40.00; C8–$25.00; C6–$10.00.
Roy Rogers and Cowboy Toby, 6⅞" x 8", Little Golden Book, copyright 1954. C10–$40.00; C8–$25.00; C6–$10.00.

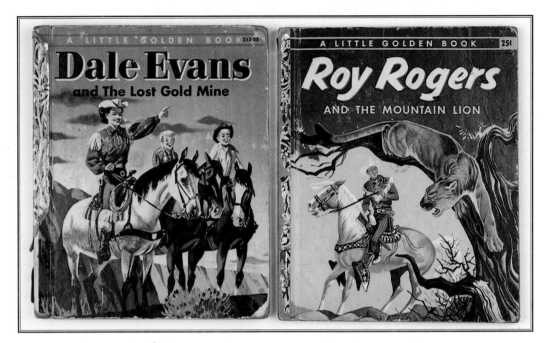

Dale Evans and the Lost Gold Mine, 6⅞" x 8", Little Golden Book, copyright 1954. C10–$40.00; C8–$25.00; C6–$10.00.

Roy Rogers and the Mountain Lion, 6⅞" x 8", Little Golden Book, copyright 1955. C10–$40.00; C8–$25.00; C6–$10.00.

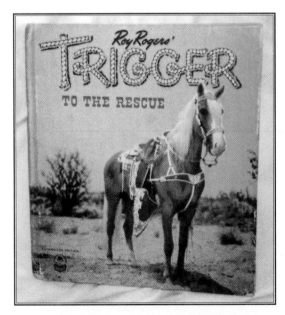

Roy Rogers' Trigger to the Rescue, 6¾" x 8", Cozy Corner Book, copyright 1950. C10–$35.00; C8–$20.00; C6–$10.00.

Roy Rogers at the Lane Ranch, 6⅞" x 8", Tell-A-Tell Book, copyright 1950. C10–$40.00; C8–$25.00; C6–$10.00.

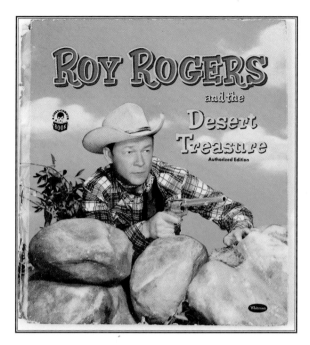

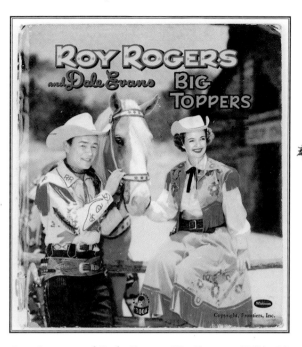

Roy Rogers and the Desert Treasure, 6⅞" x 8" Cozy Corner Book, copyright 1954. C10–$45.00; C8–$25.00; C6–$15.00.

Roy Roger and Dale Evans: Big Topper, 6⅞" x 8", Cozy Corner Book, copyright 1956. C10–$45.00; C8–$25.00; C6–$15.00.

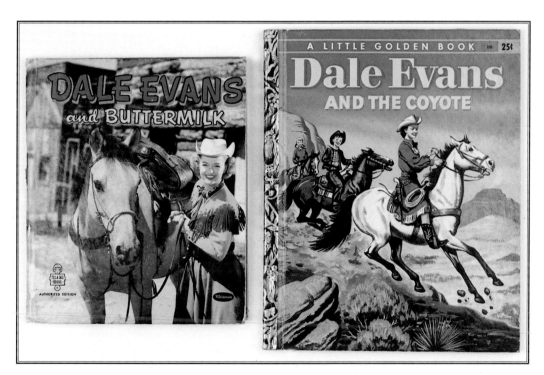

Dale Evans and Buttermilk, 6½" x 6", Tell-A-Tale Book, copyright 1956. C10–$35.00; C8–$20.00; C6–$10.00.
Dale Evans and the Coyote, 6⅞" x 8", Little Golden Book, copyright 1956. C10–$35.00; C8–$20.00; C6–$10.00.

Roy Rogers' Bullet Leads the Way, 5½" x 6½", Tell-A-Tale Book, copyright 1953. C10–$30.00; C8–$15.00; C6–$5.00.

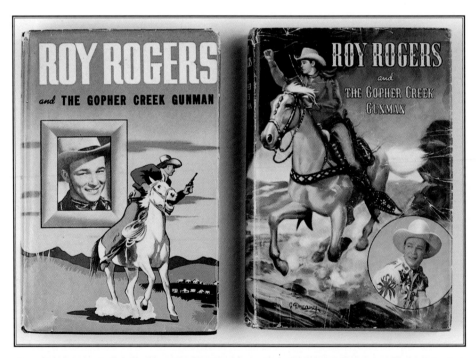

Roy Rogers and the Gopher Creek Gunman, 6" x 8", green cover with dust jacket, Whitman Publishing Co., copyright 1945. C10–$40.00; C8–$25.00; C6–$10.00.
Roy Rogers and the Gopher Creek Gunman, 6" x 8", blue cover with dust jacket, Whitman Publishing Co., copyright 1945. C10–$40.00; C8–$25.00; C6–$10.00.

Roy Rogers and the Brasada Bandits, 6" x 8", Whitman Publishing Co., copyright 1955. C10–$45.00; C8–$30.00; C6–$10.00.

Roy Rogers and Dale Evans in River of Peril, 6" x 8", Whitman Publishing Co., copyright 1957. C10–$45.00; C8–$25.00; C6–$10.00.

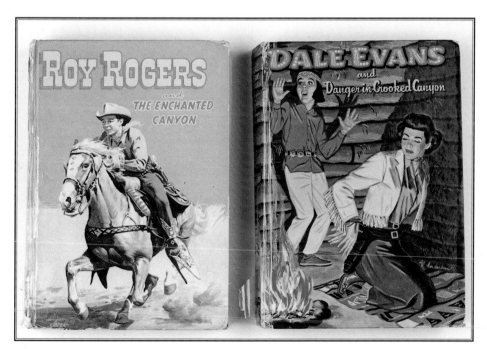

Roy Rogers and the Enchanted Canyon, 8" x 6", Whitman Publishing Co., copyright 1954. C10–$45.00; C8–$25.00; C6–$10.00.

Dale Evans and Danger In Crooked Canyon, 8" x 6", Whitman Publishing Co., copyright 1958. C10–$40.00; C8–$25.00; C6–$10.00.

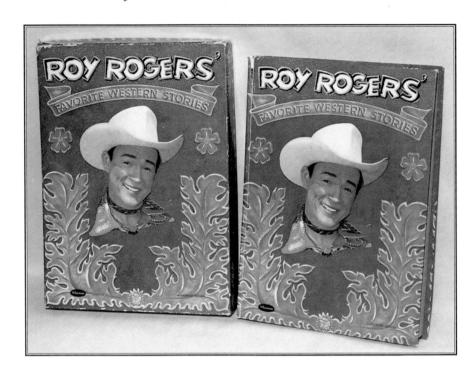

Roy Rogers Favorite Western Stories, with box 7" x 10", Whitman Publishing Co., copyright 1956. C10–$65.00; C8–$35.00; C6–$15.00; add $35.00 for box.

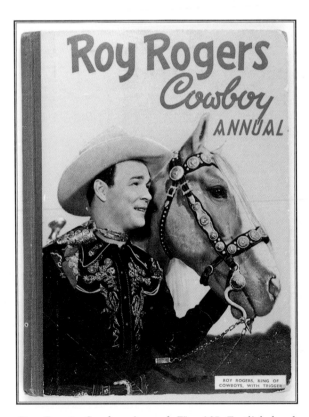

Roy Rogers Cowboy Annual, 7" x 10", English hardcover, copyright 1952. C10–$65.00; C8–$45.00; C6–$20.00.

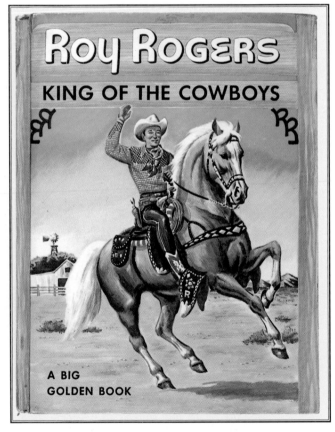

Roy Rogers: King of the Cowboys, 7" x 10", English hardcover, copyright 1950. C10–$65.00; C8–$45.00; C6–$20.00.

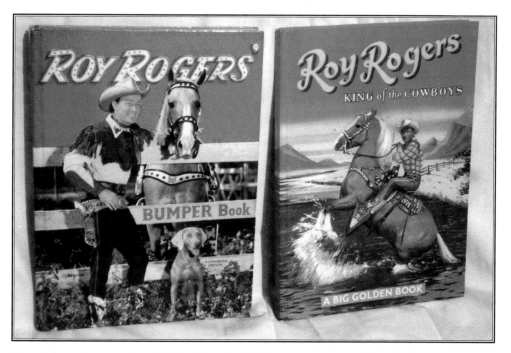

Roy Rogers Bumper Book, 7" x 10", English hardcover, copyright 1955. C10–$50.00; C8–$35.00; C6–$15.00.

Roy Rogers King of the Cowboys, A Big Golden Book, 7" x 10", English, c. 1950s. C10–$65.00; C8–$35.00; C6–$15.00.

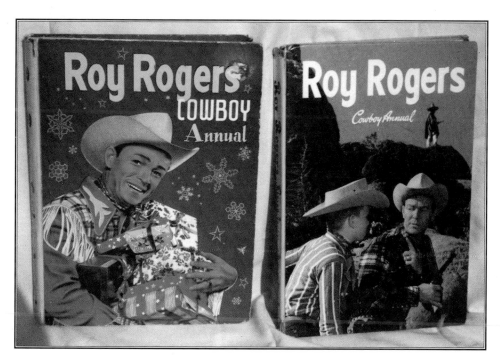

Roy Rogers Cowboy Annual #4, 7" x 10", English hardcover, copyright 1954. C10–$65.00; C8–$40.00; C6–$20.00.

Roy Rogers Cowboy Annual #11, 7" x 10", English hardcover, copyright 1961. C10–$50.00; C8–$30.00; C6–$15.00.

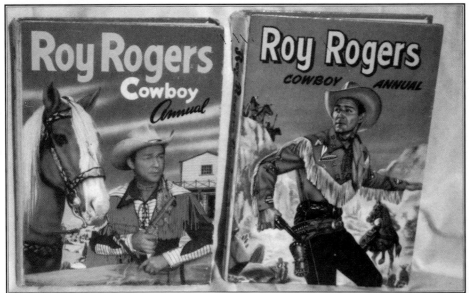

Roy Rogers Cowboy Annual, 7" x 11", English hardcover, copyright 1950s. C10–$60.00; C8–$30.00; C6–$15.00.
Roy Rogers Cowboy Annual, 7" x 11", English hardcover, copyright 1950s. C10–$60.00; C8–$30.00; C6–$15.00.

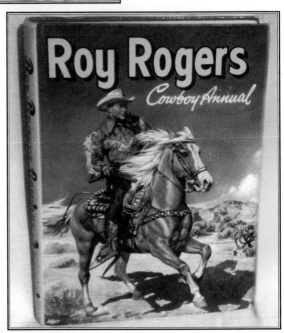

Roy Rogers Cowboy Annual #1, 7" x 11", English hardcover, copyright 1951. C10–$65.00; C8–$40.00; C6–$20.00.

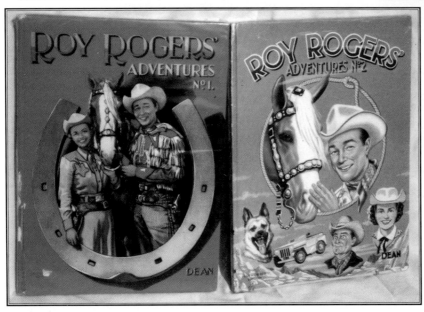

Roy Rogers Adventures No. 1, 7" x 11", English hardcover, copyright 1958. C10–$50.00; C8–$30.00; C6–$15.00.
Roy Rogers Adventures No. 2, 7" x 11", English hardcover, copyright 1959. C10–$50.00; C8–$30.00; C6–$15.00.

Lunch Boxes and Thermoses

Millions of children carried their sandwiches, cakes, cookies, milk, and soft drinks in their Roy Rogers and Dale Evans lunch box and thermos during the 50s and early 60s. Roy was the second cowboy to have his likeness depicted on a metal lunch box. Hopalong Cassidy on an Alladin lunch box was the first. But that was only a decal on a solid red or blue box. But after several attempts American Thermos was convinced to manufacture a fully lithographed steel lunch box. Lucky for American Thermos. We all know the rest is history. Over the next decade, beginning in 1953, there would be at least eight different lunch boxes and many of those with different variations. There would be primarily three different thermoses, but there would be numerous cup and cork variations.

These different variations and versions have confused a lot of collectors in the past, including myself. Hopefully this chapter will clear up some of this confusion.

As with most everything else, condition, scarcity, and demand dictates the going prices of lunch boxes and thermoses. Lunch boxes and thermoses with their original papers and stickers will most often bring the highest prices.

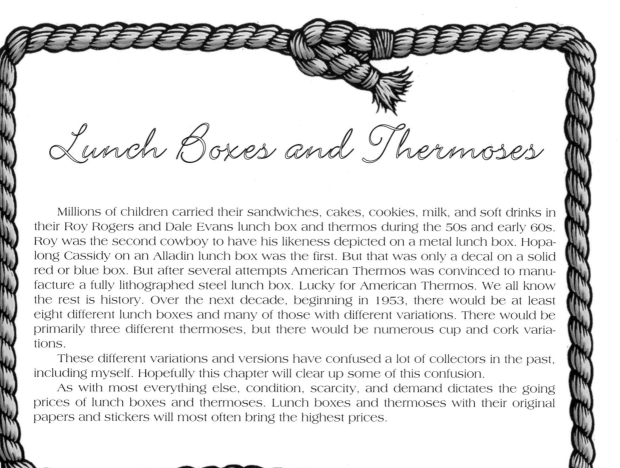

A Western Hit...
ROY ROGERS LUNCH KIT

For All School Children

Compact flat, lightweight lunch kit... fabricated of lithographed steel... side air vents... sturdy metal bottle-grasp, lock-closure and handle.

Quality half-pint bottle... double walled glass vacuum insulated filler... lithographed steel barrel... plastic cup.

Design equally appealing to boys and girls... Roy Rogers, Dale Evans, Trigger and Bullet in full color action pictures on both lunch kit and matching half-pint bottle... wood grain finish for added style appeal.

Suggested Minimum Retail Price: **$2.49**

Packed: 10 to a standard shipping carton.
Weight: 19 Lb.
Shipped: F.O.B. Norwich, Connecticut

THE AMERICAN THERMOS BOTTLE COMPANY
Norwich, Connecticut

Roy Rogers Catalog and Merchandise Manual, 1953.

Roy Rogers and Dale Evans lunch box by American Thermos, narrow woodgrain version, 6½" x 8½" x 3", came with half pint version thermos, circa 1953 – 1954. C10–$350.00; C8–$150.00; C6–$50.00.

Roy Rogers and Dale Evans, lunch box by American Thermos, 6½" x 8½" x 4", lunch box came in red and blue band versions, came with yellow background thermos or half pint thermos, circa 1954. C10–$325.00; C8–$175.00; C6–$50.00.

Roy Rogers and Dale Evans lunch box by American Thermos with leather handle, 6½" x 8½" x 4", came in red and blue versions, came with yellow sky background thermos, circa 1954. C10–$325.00; C8–$175.00; C6–$50.00.

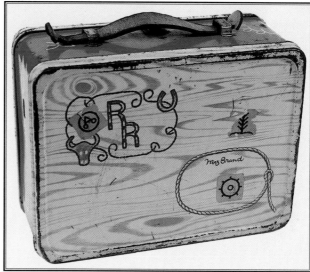

Roy Rogers and Dale Evans, lunch box by American Thermos, 6½" x 8½" x 4", eight scene version, cowhide back, came in red and green band versions, came with blue sky background thermos, circa 1956. C10–$350.00; C8–$200.00; C6–$75.00.

Roy Rogers and Dale Evans lunch box by American Thermos, 6½" x 8½" x 4", Roy on rearing Trigger front, eight scene back, came in red and green band version, came with blue sky background thermos, circa 1955. C10–$350.00; C8–$200.00; C6–$75.00.

Roy Rogers and Dale Evans Lunch Kits
Heavy gauge metal kits in full color. Flat kit has large portrait on one panel and rodeo scene on the reverse. Junior or dome type kit features Roy and Dale in the traditional chow wagon. Both kits have strong plastic handles, easy-to-clean white interiors, rust-resistant fittings, and a big 10-oz. vacuum bottle by Thermos® equipped with the exclusive Polly Red Top® closure.

Exclusive stopper features: The vacuum bottle in all kits is equipped with non-drip pouring lip and Polly Red Top® pressure seal insulated stopper so easy to put on and take off. Here's all you do: (1) Place stopper in neck opening and set cap-cup in position. (2) Tighten cap-cup firmly. Pressure seats the stopper snugly. Properly tightened, it cannot pop out or leak. (3) To remove, unscrew cap-cup and lift out stopper.

#497 — Flat School Lunch Kit & Bottle
#697 — Chow Wagon School Lunch Kit & Bottle
Retail about . . . $2.79 each

The American Thermos Products Company
Norwich, Connecticut

43

1959 – 60 catalog page 43 showing the Roy Rogers and Dale Evans Chow Wagon and Roy Rogers and Dale Evans Double R Bar Ranch lunch boxes.

Roy Rogers and Dale Evans lunch box by American Thermos, 6½" x 8½" x 4", Roy with red shirt and red lettering, came with gray band, came with yellow background thermos, circa 1957. C10–$425.00; C8–$250.00; C6–$75.00. Canadian version same but with black lettering, add $75.00 for Canadian version (not shown).

Roy Rogers and Dale Evans long dome steel chow wagon lunch box by American Thermos, 4½" x 6½" x 8½", came with yellow sky background thermos, circa 1955. C10–$450.00; C8–$275.00; C6–$100.00.

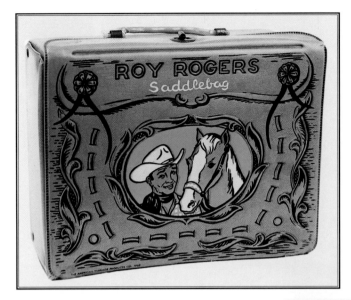

Roy Rogers vinyl lunch box by King Seely Co, 7" x 9" x 4", came in two different versions, brown and cream, came with yellow sky background Thermos, circa 1960.
Brown version: C10–$300.00; C8–$150.00; C6–$50.00.
Cream version: C10–$550.00; C8–$300.00; C6–$150.00 (rare).

Trigger steel luncheon by American Thermos, 6" x 8½" x 3", no thermos was issued with this luncheon, circa 1956.
C10–$325.00; C8–$175.00; C6–$75.00.

Examples of different thermos cork and cup variations.

Roy Rogers and Dale Evans yellow sky background thermos by American Thermos, Roy on rearing Trigger. C10–$150.00; C8–$75.00; C6–$35.00.

Roy Rogers and Dale Evans narrow half pint thermos by American Thermos, Roy, Dale, Trigger, and Bullet in front of Double R Bar Ranch entrance gate. C10–$150.00; C8–$75.00; C6–$35.00.

Roy Rogers and Dale Evans blue sky background thermos by American Thermos, Roy on rearing Trigger. C10–$175.00; C8–$75.00; C6–$35.00.

Reproduction of a 1954 Roy Rogers and Dale Evans Double R Bar Ranch lunchbox.

Reproduction of a 1957 Roy Rogers and Dale Evans Double R Bar Ranch lunchbox.

These lunch boxes are available from Arrow Catch Productions for $59.00 plus $6.50 for shipping. Call or write Arrow Catch Productions, 1029 Vernon Way, El Cajon, CA 92020, 619-562-9962.

School Supplies

Sponsors took full advantage of Roy Rogers's and Dale Evans's popularity by offering a large selection of school supplies featuring their images. This made shopping for back-to-school supplies fun. There is no doubt many items are not listed here. The intent of this chapter is to give the reader a good overview of the many school items that were available during the 1950s and early 1960s.

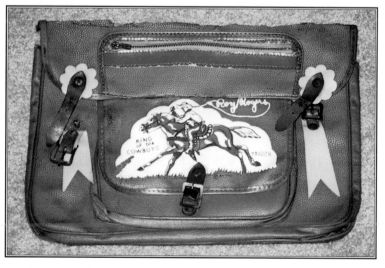

Roy Rogers and Trigger pebble-grained simulated leather school bag, 11" x 14", circa 1950. C10–$200.00; C8–$125.00; C6–$50.00.

Dale Evans school bag with shoulder strap, 14" x 9", circa 1959 –
1960. C10–$300.00; C8–$150.00; C6–$75.00.

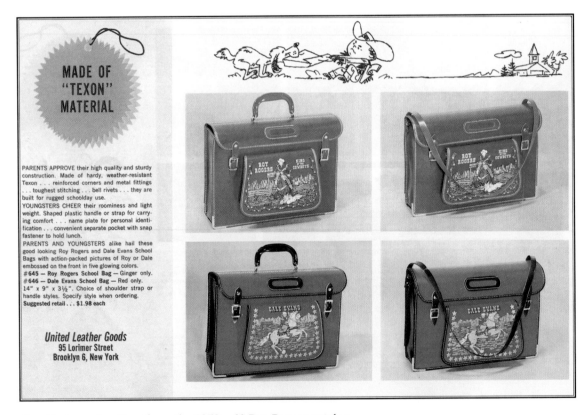

Roy Rogers school bag from the 1959 – 60 Roy Rogers catalog.

Roy Rogers and Dale Evans school bags from the 1953 Catalogue and Merchandising Manual.

Roy Rogers crayon and pencil box, 8" x 5".
C10–$125.00; C8–$75.00; C6–$35.00.

Roy Rogers red crayon and pencil box, c. 1950s. C10–$125.00; C8–$75.00; C6–$35.00.

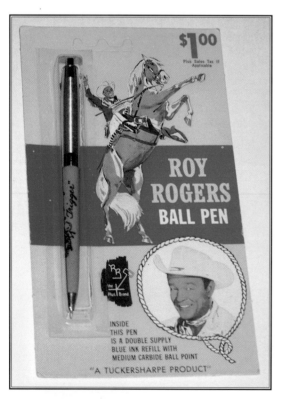

Roy Rogers ball point pen, circa 1950s. C10–$75.00; C8–$50.00; C6–$25.00; add $75.00 for original blister pack card.

Roy Rogers pencil case, circa 1950s. C10–$100.00; C8–$50.00; C6–$25.00.

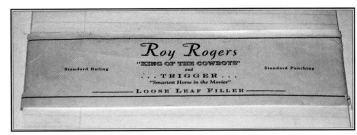

Roy Rogers and Trigger loose leaf filler notebook. C10–$30.00; C8–$20.00; C6–$10.00.

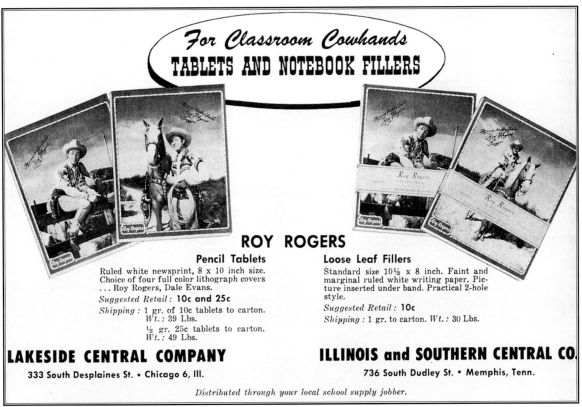

For Classroom Cowhands
TABLETS AND NOTEBOOK FILLERS

ROY ROGERS

Pencil Tablets

Ruled white newsprint, 8 x 10 inch size. Choice of four full color lithograph covers ... Roy Rogers, Dale Evans.

Suggested Retail: **10c and 25c**

Shipping: 1 gr. of 10c tablets to carton. *Wt.*: 39 Lbs.
½ gr. 25c tablets to carton. *Wt.*: 49 Lbs.

Loose Leaf Fillers

Standard size 10½ x 8 inch. Faint and marginal ruled white writing paper. Picture inserted under band. Practical 2-hole style.

Suggested Retail: **10c**

Shipping: 1 gr. to carton. *Wt.*: 30 Lbs.

LAKESIDE CENTRAL COMPANY

333 South Desplaines St. • Chicago 6, Ill.

ILLINOIS and SOUTHERN CENTRAL CO.

736 South Dudley St. • Memphis, Tenn.

Distributed through your local school supply jobber.

TOPS IN QUALITY

All youngsters need an ample supply of tablets for drawing pictures, for scribbling, or for homework if they are students. Boys and girls of any age are certain to be thrilled by these big, eye appealing pencil tablets with their wide variety of picture covers featuring natural-color autographed photos of Roy Rogers, Dale Evans, Trigger, and Bullet the Wonder Dog. The covers are ideal for framing or tacking on the wall after the pages are used up. All tablets come in the handy 8"x10" size and contain smooth-finished white newsprint stock clearly ruled in blue, with deep top margins.

Standard sheet-count size
Suggested retail . . . 10¢
Extra-large sheet-count size
Suggested retail . . . 25¢
Jumbo sheet-count size
Suggested retail . . . 39¢

DISTRIBUTED BY LOCAL SCHOOL SUPPLY JOBBERS THROUGHOUT THE UNITED STATES.

Lakeside Central Company
333 Desplaines Street
Chicago 6, Illinois
Southern Central Company
736 South Dudley Street
Memphis, Tennessee

44

Roy Rogers pencil tablets. C10–$50.00; C8–$30.00; C6–$15.00. From the 1953 and 1959–60 Roy Rogers catalogs.

91

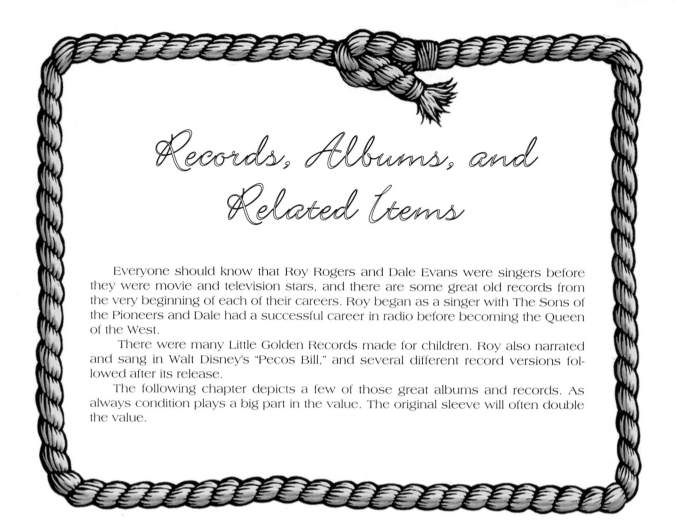

Records, Albums, and Related Items

Everyone should know that Roy Rogers and Dale Evans were singers before they were movie and television stars, and there are some great old records from the very beginning of each of their careers. Roy began as a singer with The Sons of the Pioneers and Dale had a successful career in radio before becoming the Queen of the West.

There were many Little Golden Records made for children. Roy also narrated and sang in Walt Disney's "Pecos Bill," and several different record versions followed after its release.

The following chapter depicts a few of those great albums and records. As always condition plays a big part in the value. The original sleeve will often double the value.

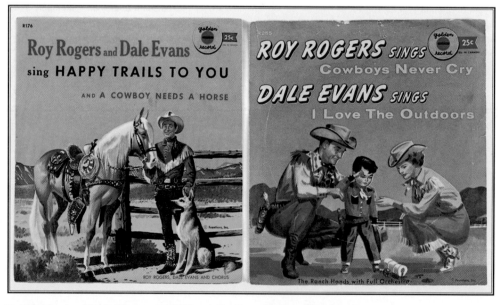

Roy Rogers and Dale Evans sing "Happy Trails to You" and "A Cowboy Needs a Horse," Little Golden Records, circa 1950s. C10–$40.00; C8–$25.00; C6–$15.00.

Roy Rogers sings "Cowboys Never Cry"; Dale Evans sings " I Love the Outdoors," Little Golden Records, c.1950s. C10–$35.00; C8–$25.00; C6–$15.00.

Roy Rogers and Dale Evans sing "Easter Is a Loving Time" and "Candy Cane Cake Walk," Little Golden Records, c. 1950s. C10–$35.00; C8–$25.00; C6–$15.00.
Roy Rogers and Dale Evans sing "Jesus Loves the Little Children" and "The Lord Is Gonna Take Good Care of You," Little Golden Records, c.1950s. C10–$35.00; C8–$25.00; C6–$15.00.

Roy Rogers sings "The Lord's Prayer"; Dale Evans sings "Ava Maria," Little Golden Records, c. 1950s. C10–$35.00; C8–$25.00; C6–$15.00.
Roy Rogers sings "Swedish Rhapsody" and "Bamboo Boat," Little Golden Records, c. 1950s. C10–$35.00; C8–$25.00; C6–$15.00.

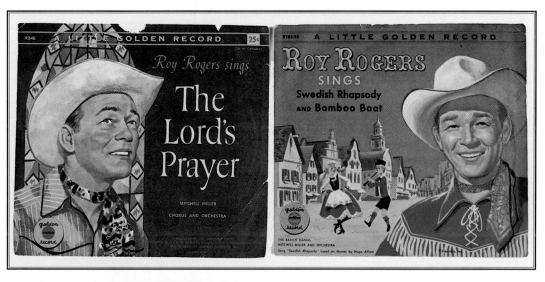

Roy Rogers and Dale Evans sing "A Good Night Prayer" and "Keep in Touch," c. 1950s. C10–$35.00; C8–$25.00; C6–$15.00.
Pat Brady sings "Roy Rogers Had a Ranch," Roy Rogers and Dale Evans sing "The Chuck Wagon Song," Little Golden Records, c. 1950s C10–$35.00; C8–$25.00; C6–$15.00.

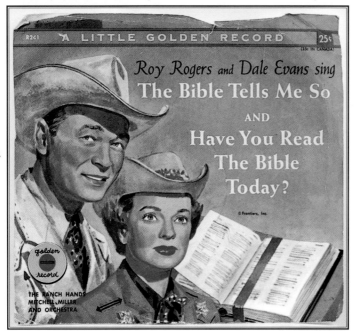

Roy Rogers and Dale Evans sing "The Bible Tells Me So" and "Have You Read The Bible Today?," Little Golden Records, c. 1950s C10–$35.00; C8–$25.00; C6–$15.00.

Roy Rogers and Dale Evans sing "The Night Before Christmas," Little Golden Records, c. 1950s. C10–$35.00; C8–$25.00; C6–$15.00.

"Roy Rogers and Dale Evans Song Wagon" includes 16 songs of the Old West, Little Golden Records, c. 1950s. C10–$200.00; C8–$100.00; C6–$50.00.

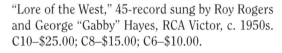

"Lore of the West," 45-record sung by Roy Rogers and George "Gabby" Hayes, RCA Victor, c. 1950s. C10–$25.00; C8–$15.00; C6–$10.00.

"Lore of the West," RCA Victor Youth Series 2, 10" dia. 78-record set in fold out sleeve depicting songs and illustrations to records, song and story by Roy Rogers and George "Gabby" Hayes, c. 1949. C10–$50.00; C8–$35.00; C6–$20.00.

"Lore of the West," RCA Victor Little Nipper Series 2, 7" dia. 45-record set in cardboard foldout sleeve depicting color illustrations of story, told in song and story by Roy Rogers and George "Gabby" Hayes, c. 1949. C10–$50.00; C8–$35.00; C6–$20.00.

95

"Skip to My Lou" and other square dances on two 7" dia. 45-record set in 7½" cardboard box, c. 1950s. C10–$35.00; C8–$25.00; C6–$15.00.

"Roy Rogers Souvenir Album" includes four 10" dia. 78-records with songs from various Roy Rogers Republic movies, in 12" x 10" cardboard sleeve, RCA Victor Musical Smart Set. C10–$65.00; C8–$40.00; C6–$20.00.

"Roy Rogers Tells and Sings about Pecos Bill" from Walt Disney's Melody Time with The Sons of the Pioneers, album includes three 10" dia. 78-records in 12" x 10" cardboard sleeved, RCA Victor Little Nipper Series, c. 1950s. C10–$75.00; C8–$50.00; C6–$25.00.

"Roy Rogers Rip Roaring Adventures of Pecos Bill," album set includes three 10" dia. 78 records in 12" x 10" cardboard sleeve, RCA Victor Youth Series, c. 1950s. C10–$75.00; C8–$50.00; C6–$25.00.

"Roy Rogers Tells and Sings about Pecos Bill," later version on LP, Camden. C10–$35.00; C8–$25.00; C6–$10.00.

Roy Rogers and Dale Evans "Christmas Is Always," Dale Evans autographed LP cover album, c. 1970s, Capitol Records. C10–$25.00; C8–$15.00; C6–$5.00; add $50.00 for autograph.

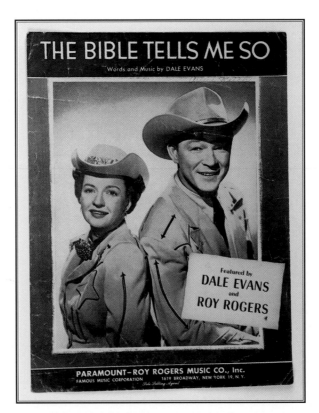

Roy Rogers and Dale Evans song folio, "The Bible Tells Me So," c. 1950s. C10–$25.00; C8–$15.00; C6–$5.00.

Miscellaneous Furnishings and Equipment

Roy Rogers and Dale Evans endorsed not only toys but also home and outdoor equipment. Kids could decorate their rooms with Roy Rogers bedspreads and drapes or spend the night outdoors in their Roy Rogers sleeping bag inside their Roy Rogers tent. One can be sure that every Roy Rogers and Dale Evans item is not listed here and there are many items yet to be discovered. For me that is what makes collecting so much fun because you never know what you might find at that next auction or antique store. Again condition is the main thing to keep in mind when purchasing these great old collectibles.

Roy Rogers and Trigger 8½" plaster lamp with engraved signature with 5½" tall original cardboard shade, c. 1950s. C10–$450.00; C8–$300.00; C6–$150.00; deduct $100.00 if missing original shade.

Dale Evans and Buttermilk 8½" plaster lamp with engraved signature with 5½" original cardboard shade, c. 1950s. C10–$500.00; C8–$325.00; C6–$175.00; deduct $100.00 if missing original shade.

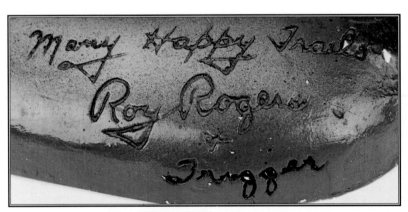

Roy Rogers and Trigger 15" plaster lamp with engraved signature (shade in photo is not original), c. 1950s. C10–$450.00; C8–$300.00; C6–150.00; deduct $100.00 if missing original shade.

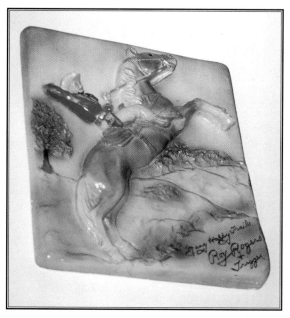

Roy Rogers and Trigger 7" x 7" x 5" plaster display, rare, origin unknown. C10–$300.00; C8–$150.00; C6–$50.00.

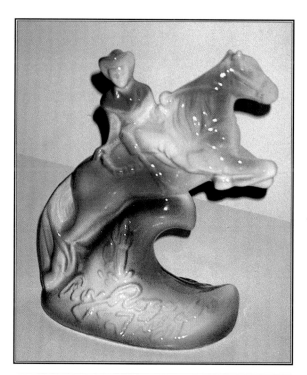

Roy Rogers and Trigger 7½" china bank with engraved Roy Rogers and Trigger signature. C10–$300.00; C8–$150.00; C6–$75.00.

Roy Rogers 6" plaster bobber head, made in Japan, c. early 1960s. C10–$300.00; C8–$150.00; C6–$75.00; add $100.00 for original shipping box.

Roy Rogers and Trigger 9" plate by Universal Co. Oven Proof. C10–$75.00; C8–$50.00; C6–$25.00.
Roy Rogers and Trigger 6" bowl by Universal Co. Oven Proof. C10–$65.00; C8–$35.00; C6–$15.00.

Roy Rogers and Trigger 5-piece chinaware set by Universal Co. Oven Proof. Includes one plate, one Roy on Trigger bowl, one Trigger bowl, and one Roy Rogers cup and saucer. Complete C10–$600.00; C8–$300.00; C6–$150.00; add $150.00 for original shipping box.

Roy Rogers gray and blue twin bedspread, c. 1950s.
C10–$175.00; C8–$100.00; C6–$50.00.

Roy Rogers brown background twin bed spread, c. 1950s. C10–$175.00;
C8–$100.00; C6–$50.00.

Roy Rogers umbrella tent by Hettrick, 72" x 72" x 60", c. 1950s. C10–$200.00; C8–$150.00; C6–$75.00; add $100.00 for original box and accessories.

PLAY VALUE AND UTILITY

#8686 — Roy Rogers Chuck Wagon
Wagon-cycle with 16" ball-bearing front wheel and 8" rear disc wheels with plated hub caps; 1¾" semi-pneumatic tires; bicycle-type fenders; adjustable tubular steel handlebar with rubber grips; block rubber pedals; adjustable saddle with simulated leather finish. The steel wagon body has a white canvas cover decorated on both sides.
Suggested retail . . . $19.95

#K-409 — Roy Rogers Sleeping Bag
Designed with eye appeal and built for warmth and comfort. A roomy 24" x 54", it is made of moistureproof vinyl, well-filled and lined with soft kasha cloth. It closes easily with two heavy snap fasteners. For that extra touch to give the outdoors all the comforts of home, there is an individual 10" x 16" pneumatic pillow.
Suggested retail . . . $5.50

The Hettrick Mfg. Co.
Summit at Magnolia Sts.
Toledo 1, Ohio

#K-153 — Roy Rogers Tepee Tent
Just right for "playing Indians" is this tepee tent made of durable, painted 4-oz. fabric. Finished size is 54" x 54", center height of 51", and a 23" x 36" awning extension. Complete with sturdy wood center pole and awning extension poles, ropes, and stakes.
Suggested retail . . . $5.95

#K-152 — Roy Rogers Umbrella Tent
Roomy play or camping tent of quality 4-oz. fabric. Finished size is 72" x 72", center height of 60", with 45" walls, 32" x 50" combination door-awning, and 30" square eaves supported by a special wire frame. Complete with a full set of ropes, poles, and stakes.
Suggested retail . . . $10.95

#329 — Roy Rogers Clubhouse Play Tent
All young cowpokes hanker for secret hide-aways. There is just such a concealed secret door in the rear of this clubhouse play tent. Made of special tent cloth, it measures 42" x 42", with 39" walls, and comes complete, ready to set up.
Suggested retail . . . $12.98

Roy Rogers sleeping bag, 24" x 54", c. 1950s. C10–$175.00; C8–$125.00; C6–$50.00.
Roy Rogers Clubhouse Play Tent by Hettrick, c. 1950s. C10–$250.00; C8–$175.00; C6–$100.00.
Roy Rogers Tepee tent by Hettrick, 54" x 54", c. 1950s. C10–$175.00; C8–$125.00; C6–$50.00.
Roy Rogers Chuck Wagon tricycle, c. 1950s, original. C10–$1,500.00 – 2,000.00. 1959–1960 catalog.
Also shown Roy Rogers umbrella tent.

A Western World of Their Own
ROY ROGERS RANCH ITEMS

Roy Rogers Bunk House No. 55

Their own hide-out. Made of select kiln-dried lumber. Clinch nailed on sturdy backing strips. Roof of weather-proof hardboard; supported by sturdy stripping. Easy-to-assemble five sections. Particularly designed to weather well and give many years of outdoor service, with or without additional painting. *Size:* 60" wide x 40" deep — front 59" high, back 48" high.
Packed: 1 unit to a carton.
Shipping Weight: 100 Lbs.

Suggested Retail: **$34.95**

Roy Rogers Ranch Gate   No. 57

Sturdy, junior-size duplicate of Roy's own Ranch Gate. *Size:* 6' wide x 5½' high x 2¼" thick. *Shipping Weight:* 30 Lbs.

Suggested Retail: **$18.95**

Roy Rogers Ranch Fence   No. 56

To fence in their Western world. Kiln-dried stock. *Size:* 6' x 2' high. *Packed:* 2 to a carton. *Shipping Weight:* 12 Lbs.

Suggested Retail: **$6.50**

Roy Rogers Chair   No. 1462

Comfort all-around... before the television set, in their room, or out in their Bunk House... it's the Roy Rogers Chair. Decorated with Saddle Tan brands and Roy Rogers design on Desert Sand plastic covering... blonde lacquer finish. Long-wearing kiln-dried frame, glued and dowelled... no-sag spring seat and back filled with sisal, cotton and tufflex. *Size:* seat 16" x 16", back 25" high. *Packed:* 1 to a carton. *Shipping Weight:* 30 Lbs.

Suggested Retail: **$14.50**

LES BROWN COMPANY, INC.
Naperville, Illinois

Roy Rogers Bunkhouse and Ranch Gate. Prices unknown.
Roy Rogers child's chair, 25". C10–$600.00; C8–$300.00; C6–$150.00.
Also shown: Roy Rogers Ranch Fence.
1953 Merchandising Catalog.

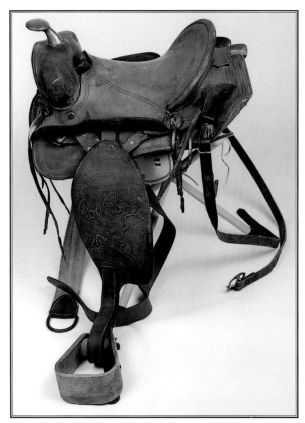

Roy Rogers tooled leather pony saddle, c. 1950s. C10–$750.00; C8–$350.00; C6–$150.00.

For the Young Cowhand
A REAL SADDLE

Built on a sturdy tree, of select saddle leather, pleasingly decorated and colored Golden Palomino — has an 11″ seat length — to fit cow waddies of all sizes. Bridle and Martingale to match are available.

Packed 1 to carton.
Shipping wt. approximately 18 lbs.

Sold through jobbers only.
Write for name of nearest distributor.

No. 508 The "ROY ROGERS"

Made by
BONA ALLEN, INC.
Buford, Georgia

1953 Merchandising Catalog.

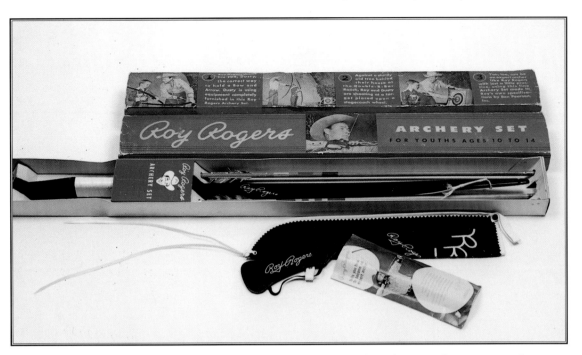

Roy Rogers boxed archery set, includes black 4½" long Hickory bow, four wooden arrows, quiver, arm guard, and instruction booklet. Complete C10–$350.00; C8–$250.00; C6–$100.00.

Roy Rogers boxed 16mm film. C10–$125.00; C8–$75.00; C6–$35.00.

Roy Rogers black leather dog collar with Roy Rogers inscribed with red stones. C10–$150.00; C8–$100.00; C6–$50.00.

Dale Evans 4" x 4" metal sewing kit box, c. 1950s. C10–$100.00; C8–$65.00; C6–$35.00.

Roy Rogers 4" x 5" wooden backed metal newspaper printers block for "Bells of Rosa Rita." C10–$150.00; C8–$75.00; C6–$40.00.

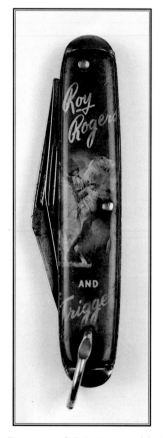

Roy Rogers and Trigger two-bladed pocket knife by Colonial Knife Co., early 1950s. C10–$200.00; C8–$100.00; C6–$50.00.

Roy Rogers 3½" (closed) three-bladed pocket knife with raised gold-plated Roy on rearing Trigger by Ulster Knife Co. C10–$300.00; C8–$150.00; C6–$75.00.

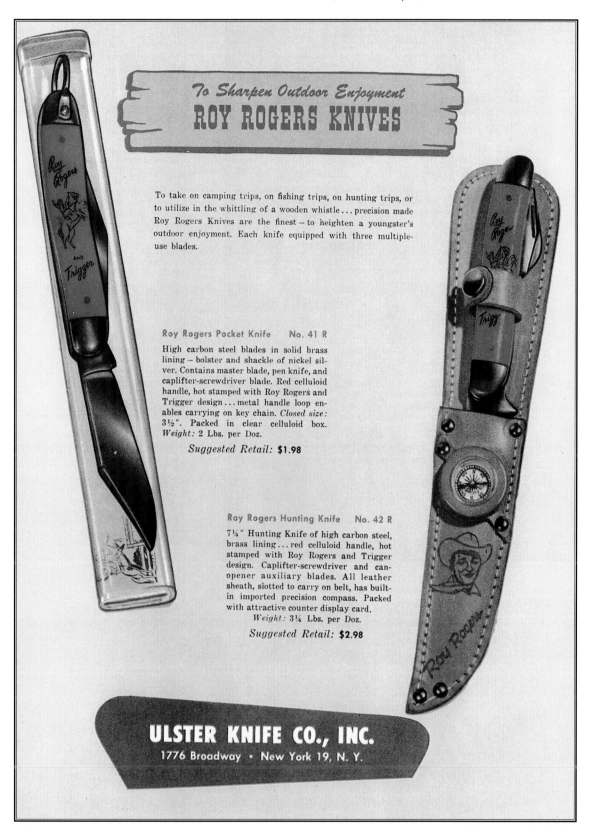

To Sharpen Outdoor Enjoyment
ROY ROGERS KNIVES

To take on camping trips, on fishing trips, on hunting trips, or to utilize in the whittling of a wooden whistle... precision made Roy Rogers Knives are the finest — to heighten a youngster's outdoor enjoyment. Each knife equipped with three multiple-use blades.

Roy Rogers Pocket Knife   No. 41 R

High carbon steel blades in solid brass lining — bolster and shackle of nickel silver. Contains master blade, pen knife, and caplifter-screwdriver blade. Red celluloid handle, hot stamped with Roy Rogers and Trigger design... metal handle loop enables carrying on key chain. *Closed size:* 3½". Packed in clear celluloid box. *Weight:* 2 Lbs. per Doz.

Suggested Retail: **$1.98**

Roy Rogers Hunting Knife   No. 42 R

7¼" Hunting Knife of high carbon steel, brass lining... red celluloid handle, hot stamped with Roy Rogers and Trigger design. Caplifter-screwdriver and can-opener auxiliary blades. All leather sheath, slotted to carry on belt, has built-in imported precision compass. Packed with attractive counter display card. *Weight:* 3¼ Lbs. per Doz.

Suggested Retail: **$2.98**

ULSTER KNIFE CO., INC.
1776 Broadway • New York 19, N. Y.

Roy Rogers 3½" two-bladed pocket knife. C10–$300.00; C8–$150.00; C6–$75.00; add $75.00 for clear celluloid box.

Roy Rogers 7¼" hunting knife with all leather sheath with compass, rare. C10–$500.00; C8–$250.00; C6–$125.00.

1953 Merchandising Catalog.

Roy Rogers and Dale Evans 21" x 15" original water color by Jonni Hill, 1996. C10-$300.00 print only.

Knock-off trash can. C10–$50.00; C8–$35.00; C6–$15.00.

ADD "TRIGGER"
TO YOUR SALES FORCE...

The original mechanical "Trigger"... safe, lively saddle rider complete with genuine leather Roy Rogers saddle and bridle... is a proven money-making traffic stopper. Manufactured by Exhibit Supply, motor driven, coin operated, with gait regulated by reins. Same model used in the famous Roy Rogers "3-R" promotion scheduled for fall.

SPECIFICATIONS:

Overall height 54". Height at saddle 45". Overall length 69". Width 20". Base 48" long, 14" wide. Powered by AC ⅓ h.p. capacitor type motor, 115 volt, 60 cycles. Weight, approx. 360 lbs. Shipping weight, approx. 400 lbs. Will accommodate rider up to 350 lbs. with ease. Roy Rogers genuine leather western saddle and trim. 10c coin chute. One minute ride. Color: Golden Palomino.

And REMEMBER Trigger is installed by a local operator without any investment by you.

COMPLETE WITH TESTED MERCHANDISE DISPLAY MATERIAL AND SALES AIDS

Write or wire

EXHIBIT SUPPLY
4218 West Lake Street · Chicago 24, Illinois

68

Roy Rogers and Trigger 10-cent ride, c. 1953, rare. Value unknown. 1953 Merchandising Manual.

WESTERN PUPPET THEATRE: 2' x 2'. . . with music!

CHUCKWAGON: 2' x 4'. Rides two

TRIGGER: 2' x 6'

NELLYBELLE: 2' x 4'. Rides two

STAGECOACH: 2' x 6'4". Rides two

Children's 10 cent rides and puppet theatre, rare. Values unknown. 1959–1960 catalog.

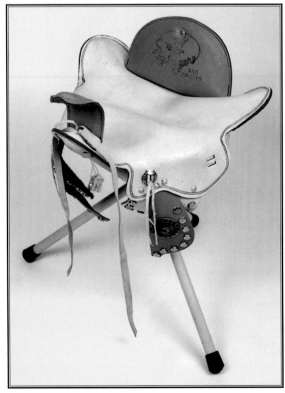

Roy Rogers 18" high child's TV saddle chair supported by three wooden legs. C10–$350.00; C8–$250.00; C6–$100.00.

Movie Posters

The King of the Cowboys starred in nearly 100 films beginning with *Under Western Stars* for Republic Pictures in 1938. He also starred in earlier films under the name Dick Weston and his birth name Len Slye. Posters for any of these classic Roy Rogers westerns are in great demand and unfortunately are fairly difficult to locate. And when you do find one they will usually have a pretty hefty price tag. Due to the number of posters and lobby cards that were generated during Roy Rogers's reign as king, it would be nearly impossible to list and illustrate each one. Unfortunately I have only a few listed in this chapter.

Roy Rogers 23" x 17" lobby card backdrop poster, c. 1950s (lobby card would be pinned/fastened to red area of backdrop poster). C10–$75.00; C8- $50.00; C6–$25.00.

Roy Rogers 23" x 17" lobby card backdrop poster, c. 1950s (lobby card would be pinned/fastened to gate area of backdrop poster). C10–$75.00; C8–$50.00; C6–$25.00.

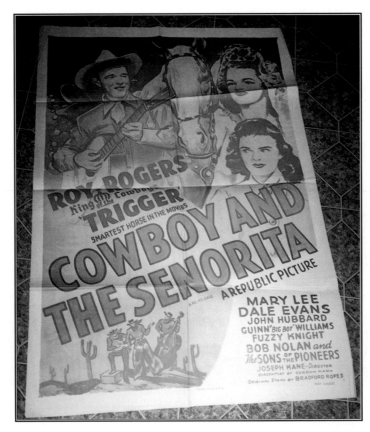

Roy Rogers, Dale Evans, and Trigger 41" x 27", 1952 re-release *Cowboy and the Senorita* movie poster. C10–$250.00; C8–$150.00; C6–$75.00; add $350.00 for original 1944 release.

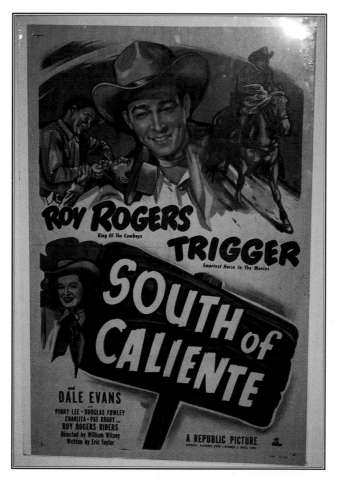

Roy Rogers, Dale Evans, and Trigger, *South of Caliente* movie poster, 41" x 27", 1951 release. C10–$500.00; C8–$300.00; C6–$150.00.

Roy Rogers and Trigger six-sheet movie poster of *On the Old Spanish Trail*. C10–$550.00; C8–$350.00; C6–$200.00.

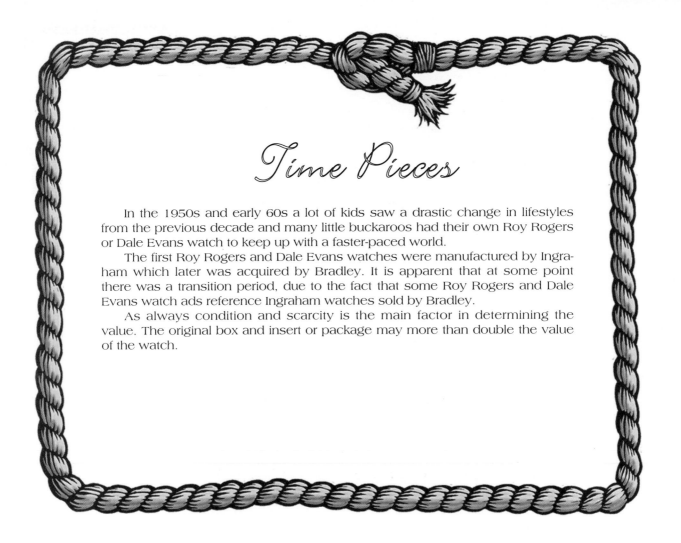

Time Pieces

In the 1950s and early 60s a lot of kids saw a drastic change in lifestyles from the previous decade and many little buckaroos had their own Roy Rogers or Dale Evans watch to keep up with a faster-paced world.

The first Roy Rogers and Dale Evans watches were manufactured by Ingraham which later was acquired by Bradley. It is apparent that at some point there was a transition period, due to the fact that some Roy Rogers and Dale Evans watch ads reference Ingraham watches sold by Bradley.

As always condition and scarcity is the main factor in determining the value. The original box and insert or package may more than double the value of the watch.

Roy Rogers wrist watch by Ingraham, c.1951. C10–$200.00; C8–$100.00; C6–$50.00; add $200.00 for original box.

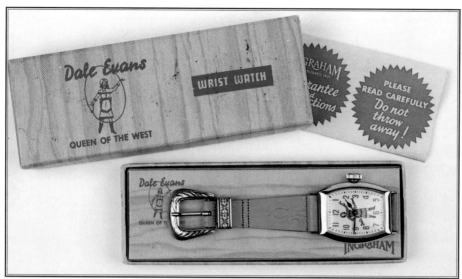

Dale Evans wrist watch by Ingraham, c. 1950s. C10–$250.00; C8–$150.00; C6–$75.00; add $250.00 for original box and papers.

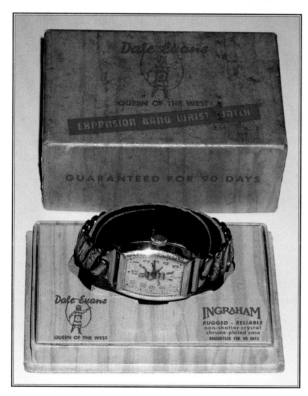

Dale Evans wrist watch with expandable metal band, c. 1950s. C10–$200.00; C8–$100.00; C6–$50.00; add $200.00 for original box.

Roy Rogers 2" dia. metal case pocket stop watch by Bradley Time, c.1950s. C10–$400.00; C8–$300.00; C6–$150.00; add $200.00 for original box.

Roy Rogers and Dale Evans wrist watch with live action face by Bradley, late 1950s. C10–$200.00; C8–$100.00; C6–$50.00; add $250.00 for rare original pop up box.
Roy Rogers Time Teacher toy watch. C10–$75.00; C8–$50.00; C6–$25.00; add $100.00 for backing card.
Also shown: Roy Rogers Binoculars.

Roy Rogers cuff links and tie clasp or Dale Evans necklace add $50.00 to value of Roy Rogers wrist watch with live action face.

Advertisement for Roy Rogers boys' wrist watches and Dale Evans girls' wrist watches, 1950s catalog.

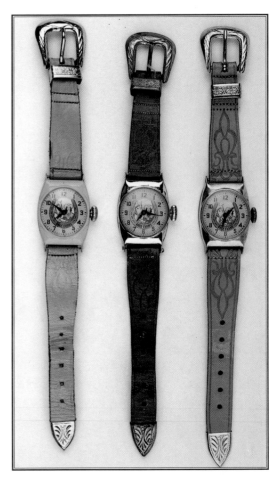

Roy Rogers round face wrist watch by Bradley, c.1950s. C10–$250.00; C8–$125.00; C6–$50.00.
Roy Rogers round wrist watch by Ingraham. C10–$200.00; C8–$125.00; C6–$50.00.

Dale Evans round face with turquoise case and band by Ingraham. C10–$225.00; C8–$150.00; C6–$75.00.
Dale Evans round face chrome-plated wrist watch by Ingraham. C10–$200.00; C8–$125.00; C6–$50.00.
Dale Evans round gold finish wrist watch by Ingraham. C10–$250.00; C8–$175.00; C6–$75.00.

Roy Rogers rectangular face wrist watch by Ingraham. C10–$200.00; C8–$100.00; C6–$50.00.

Rectangular wrist watch with Roy Rogers & Trigger engraved on expandable band, c.1950s. C10–$300.00; C8–$150.00; C6–$75.00. Wrist watch with live action with expandable metal band, Roy Rogers and Trigger engraved on watch back plate. C10–$200.00; C8–$125.00; C6–$50.00.

Dale Evans gold-plated wrist watch by Ingraham, band in photo is not original. C10–$225.00; C8–$150.00; C6–$75.00; deduct $50.00, if band is not original.

Roy Rogers and Dale Evans 1995 limited edition collector's watch set, includes tin lunch box container with Roy Rogers and Dale Evans slide tie. C10–$100.00.

Roy Rogers and Trigger alarm clock by Ingraham Co., c. 1950s, came in desert sand, cactus green, light blue. C10–$350.00; C8–$250.00; C6–$150.00; add $200.00 for original box; deduct $100.00 without Roy Rogers signature. Add $200.00 for the rare Canadian version (not shown) which came in red with numbers shown with twigs.

Cereal Premiums and Related Items

In the 50s Roy Rogers and Dale Evans were associated with many food products, including Post Raisin Bran, Quaker Oats, and Nestlés Quick to name a few. Of course the marketing strategies were to attract the little buckaroos, and it worked. Today you can find thousands of great cereal premiums to prove it. Kids would see Roy's or Dale's picture on the cereal box and have to have the neat metal litho ring or badge inside each box. Thousands of little guys would send in their box tops with 35 cents to get their authentic Roy Rogers figural cup.

Due to the many cereal premiums and related items that were given away, there are sure to be many not mentioned in this section. Prices have seen a steady increase over the past five years, but due to the introduction of the Internet some prices have leveled off in the past year or so.

1954 cereal box ad for Roy Rogers buttons.

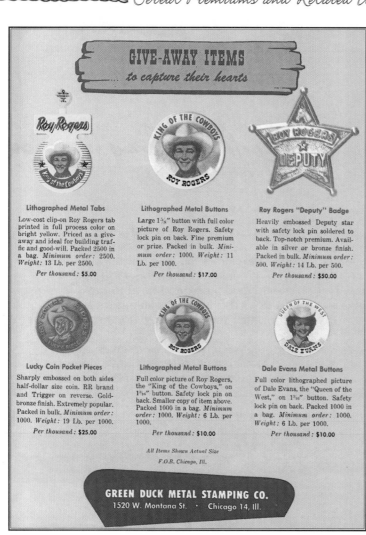

1953 catalog page showing give-away items available to retailers.

Roy Rogers large button, reads "Grapenuts Flakes" on back, worn with beanie, 1953. C10–$40.00; C8–$25.00; C6–$15.00.
Dale Evans and Trigger button, blank backs, complete set contains 15, 1953. C10–$20.00; C8–$12.00; C6–$8.00 each.

Roy's RR Bran, Post Raisin Bran tin litho ring. C10–$40.00; C8–$20.00; C6–$10.00.

Roy Rogers Post Raisin Bran tin litho ring, complete set contains 10, 1953. C10–$50.00; C8–$30.00; C6–$15.00.

Bullet, Post Raisin Bran tin litho medal, complete set contains 27, 1953. C10–$25.00; C8–$15.00; C6–$8.00.

Trigger, Post Raisin Bran tin litho medal. C10–$25.00; C8–$15.00; C6–$8.00.

Roy Rogers, Post Raisin Bran tin litho medal. C10–$40.00; C8–$25.00; C6–$10.00.

Dale Evans, Post Raisin Bran tin litho medal. C10–$35.00; C8–$20.00; C6–$10.00.

Buttermilk, Post Raisin Bran tin litho medal. C10–$25.00; C8–$15.00; C6–$8.00.

Dale Evans Gun, Post Raisin Bran tin litho medal. C10–$25.00; C8–$15.00; C6–$8.00.

Roy's Brand, Post Raisin Bran tin litho medal. C10–$25.00; C8–$15.00; C6–$8.00.

Dale's Brand, Post Raisin Bran tin litho medal C10–$25.00; C8–$15.00; C6–$8.00.

Dry Gulch, Post Raisin Bran tin litho medal. C10–$20.00; C8–$12.00; C6–$5.00.
Chuck Wagon, Post Raisin Bran tin litho medal. C10–$20.00; C8–$12.00; C6–$5.00.
Bronco Buster, Post Raisin Bran tin litho medal. C10–$20.00; C8–$12.00; C6–$5.00.
Double R Bar Rodeo, Post Raisin Bran tin litho medal. C10–$20.00; C8–$12.00; C6–$5.00.
Roy's Boots, Post Raisin Bran tin litho medal. C10–$25.00; C8–$15.00; C6–$8.00.

Sheriff's Gun, Post Raisin Bran tin litho medal. C10–$20.00; C8–$12.00; C6–$5.00.
Mule Skinner, Post Raisin Bran tin litho medal. C10–$20.00; C8–$12.00; C6–$5.00.
Indian Chief, Post Raisin Bran tin litho medal. C10–$20.00; C8–$12.00; C6–$5.00.
Deputy Marshall, Post Raisin Bran tin litho medal. C10–$20.00; C8–$12.00; C6–$5.00.
Roy Rogers Saddle, Post Raisin Bran tin litho medal. C10–$25.00; C8–$12.00; C6–$8.00.

Sheriff, Post Raisin Bran tin litho medal. C10–$20.00; C8–$12.00; C6–$5.00.
Rodeo Stunt Rider, Post Raisin Bran tin litho medal. C10–$20.00; C8–$12.00; C6–$5.00.
U.S. Marshall, Post Raisin Bran tin litho medal. C10–$20.00; C8–$12.00; C6–$5.00.
Ranch Foreman, Post Raisin Bran tin litho medal. C10–$20.00; C8–$12.00; C6–$5.00.
Nellybelle, Post Raisin Bran tin litho medal. C10–$20.00; C8–$12.00; C6–$5.00.

Pocket-size Post Cereals puzzle, 1957, set of six. C10–$30.00; C8–$20.00; C6–$10.00 each.

Post cereal pop out cards, set of 36, from 1952. C10–$25.00; C8–$10.00; C6–$5.00 each.

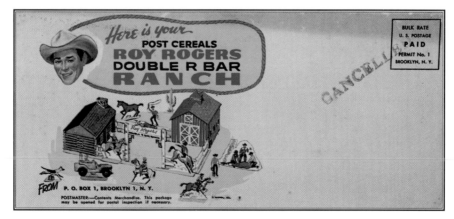

Post Cereals Roy Rogers Ranch, all cardboard, 1955. C10–$35.00; C8–$15.00; C6–$10.00.

Roy Rogers Ranch set, Post Cereals store poster, 21" x 22", 1955. C10–$300.00; C8–$150.00; C6–$75.00.

Roy Rogers Double R Bar Ranch set, metal Nellybelle, plastic figures, punch outs with box, and instructions sheet, rare. C10–$500.00; C8–$300.00; C6–$150.00.

Quaker three pound canister with souvenir cup offer, 1950. C10–$85.00; C8–$40.00; C6–$20.00.
Roy Rogers plastic mug by F&F Mold and Die Works Dayton, Ohio. C10–$35.00; C8–$20.00; C6–$10.00.

Mother's Oats (Quaker Oats) three pound canister with Roy Rogers Branding Iron ring offer, 1950s. C10–$85.00; C8–$40.00; C6–$20.00.
Mother's Oats (Quaker Oats) one pound, four ounces canister with Roy Rogers Deputy Sheriff's Badge offer, 1950s. C10–$75.00; C8–$35.00; C6–$15.00.

Roy Rogers Post Sugar Crisp 3-D glasses and cards, 1953. C10–$15.00;
C8–$10.00; C6–$5.00 each.

Quaker contest prize, 19" x 26" Roy Rogers and Trigger
poster, 1949, rare. C10–$1,000.00; C8–$500.00;
C6–$200.00; add $350.00 with mailer tube.

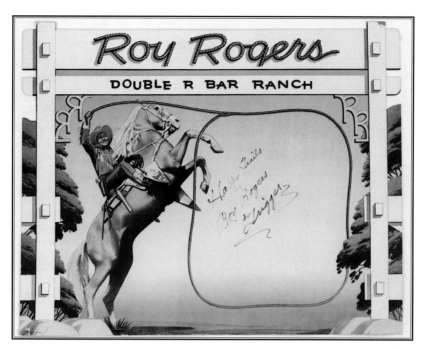

Roy Rogers 16" x 20" die cut easeled window store display, 1953. C10–$200.00; C8–$125.00; C6–$65.00; add $100.00 with Roy Rogers's autograph.

1953 catalog.

Roy Rogers Schwinn bicycles mailer advertiser, folds out, includes other Hollywood stars, 1950s. C10–$50.00; C8–$30.00; C6–$15.00.

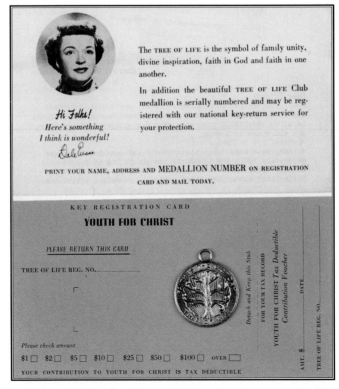

Dale Evans Youth For Christ Medal and mailer cards, 1960s.
C10–$25.00; C8–$15.00; C6–$5.00.

Roy Rogers and Dale Evans 3½" x 2¾" Christian cards, backs have Roy and Dale testimonies for children, by American Tract Society, 1950s. C10–$20.00; C8–$10.00; C6–$5.00 each.

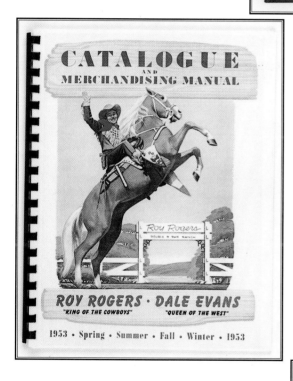

Roy Rogers 1953 Catalogue and Merchandising Manual. ALERT: This manual has been reproduced and unfortunately the reproductions have been sold as originals. The originals have a wire loop binder. Reproductions will often have a plastic loop binder. Original C10–$500.00+; C8–$300.00; C6–$150.00. Reproductions $50.00.

Roy Rogers 1959 – 1960 catalogue. C10–$500.00+;   C8–$300.00; C6–$150.00. Reproduction, $50.00.

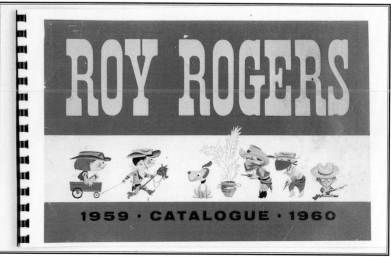

Roy Rogers Wild West action toy punch out sheet by Roy Rogers Cookies, c.1950s. Unpunched C10–$175.00; C8–$125.00; C6–$50.00.

Roy Rogers Riders Club membership kit, includes comic, membership card, and litho tin tab, 1950s. Complete, C10–$250.00; C8–$150.00; C6–$75.00.

Yellow Records mailer, 1950s. C10–$50.00; C8–$30.00; C6–$15.00.

Roy Rogers Quaker microscope ring, c. 1950s. C10–$200.00; C8–$100.00; C6–$50.00.
Roy Rogers inscribed sterling cowboy hat ring, c. 1950s, scarce (not shown). $300.00 – $750.00.
Roy Rogers branding iron ring (not shown). $100.00 – $250.00.
Roy Rogers inscribed saddle ring (not shown). $200.00 – $500.00.

Roy Rogers and Dale Evans Fan Club membership card and cello button, c. 1950s. C10–$100.00; C8–$50.00; C6–$25.00.

Roy Rogers miniature holster with generic gun and rodeo souvenir button. C10–$75.00; C8–$40.00; C6–$20.00.

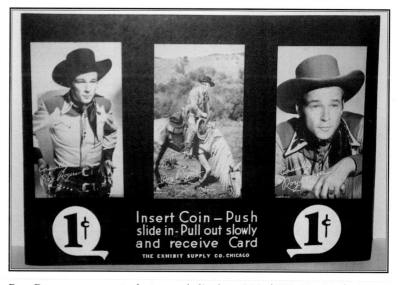

Roy Rogers one-cent photo card display. C10–$250.00; C8–$150.00; C6–$75.00.

Roy Rogers sidekick George "Gabby" Hayes, 16" x 21" paper store sign, hat, c.1951.   C10–$300.00; C8–$175.00; C6–$75.00.

Roy Rogers Kentucky State Fair Program, 1958. C10–$50.00; C8–$30.00; C6–$15.00.

Roy Rogers Restaurant paper soft drink cup and french fries holder, 1990s. $5.00 – $10.00 each.

Effective... Attractive
PERMANENT DISPLAYS

R-6 GIANT SEPIA REARING HORSE BLOW-UP

40"x 60" blow-up of Roy Rogers rearing Trigger. Reproduced in a deep, rich sepia tone and heavy paper stock. Coated with a protective finish on the surface. May be wiped with damp cloth. *Packed one to a mailing tube.*

Each **$2.25**

R-7 Standard Sepia Rearing Horse Blow-Up 30"x 40"

Packed one to a mailing tube.

Each **$1.50**

R-3 LIFE SIZE ROY ROGERS CUT-OUT

73" high, full color enlargement from a natural color photograph. Mounted on heavy board and die-cut to outline of figure. Furnished with heavy double wing easel. Rigid, will stand abuse, and extremely realistic. *Packed one to a carton.*

Each **$7.50**

R-4 Junior Size Roy Rogers Cut-Out 60" High

Packed one to a carton.

Each **$4.75**

R-2 ROGDEN MECHANICAL REARING HORSE

32" high, 30" wide, 10" deep. Trigger descends about half way from vertical... concealed light flashes on in corner of fence and stays lighted while Trigger rears to a vertical position. Produced in natural color on heavy board. Long lasting, foolproof, pendulum motor. *Packed one to a carton.*

Each **$14.75**

R-5 ROY ROGERS AND TRIGGER PLAQUES

29" in diameter, full color reproductions of Roy Rogers and Trigger. Background simulates weather beaten wood with rope border. Mounted on heavy board with hanger on back. *Packed 1 ea. Roy and Trigger to a carton.*

Each Set **$5.50**

THE ROGDEN CO.
466 West Superior St. • Chicago 10, Ill.

All prices F.O.B. Chicago

To discover one of these items would be a Roy Rogers collector's dream come true. Who knows if any of these displays still exist. Values unknown because items are so rare. 1953 Merchandising Manual.

Cowboy and Cowgirl Attire

In the 50s and early 60s nothing made a little cowboy or cowgirl prouder than strutting around in their authentic Roy Rogers or Dale Evans outfit with their guns in hand. There were many companies who manufactured these great outfits and in this chapter you will see many that were available. Roy and Dale not only had their names on these outfits, but they also endorsed ties, watches, socks, boots, etc.

In this chapter you will see many great old illustrations taken from the 1953 and 1959 – 1960 Roy Rogers and Dale Evans Merchandising Manuals. These manuals and catalogs were distributed to major retail stores throughout the United States and Canada.

Again, mint items with their original boxes and tags will bring higher prices. These items have seen a steady increase in prices throughout the 90s, but due to the current availability of these items on the Internet, the C6 through C8 condition items have seen a slight decrease in price, but the near mint to mint items still maintain their high price values.

From 1959 – 1960 catalog. This plaster Roy on Trigger has reached $4,500.00 on an Internet auction.

Child's all wool cap with inner liner earflap, Canada, rare, c. 1950s. C10–$300.00; C8–$150.00; C6–$75.00.

Roy Rogers black cowboy hat, c. 1950s. C10–$100.00; C8–$60.00; C6–$25.00.

1959 – 1960 catalog.

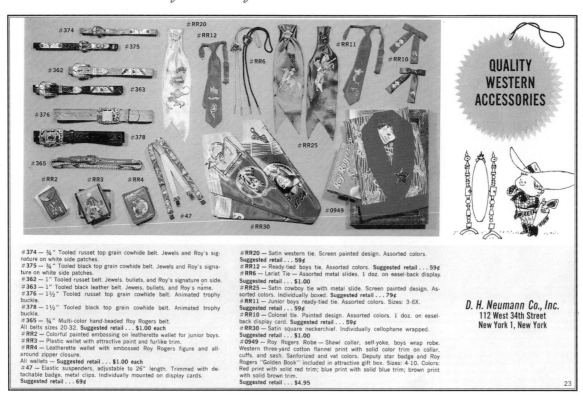

#374 — ¾" Tooled russet top grain cowhide belt. Jewels and Roy's signature on white side patches.
#375 — ¾" Tooled black top grain cowhide belt. Jewels and Roy's signature on white side patches.
#362 — 1" Tooled russet belt. Jewels, bullets, and Roy's signature on side.
#363 — 1" Tooled black leather belt. Jewels, bullets, and Roy's name.
#376 — 1½" Tooled russet top grain cowhide belt. Animated trophy buckle.
#378 — 1½" Tooled black top grain cowhide belt. Animated trophy buckle.
#365 — ¾" Multi-color hand-beaded Roy Rogers belt.
All belts sizes 20-32. **Suggested retail . . . $1.00 each**
#RR2 — Colorful painted embossing on leatherette wallet for junior boys.
#RR3 — Plastic wallet with attractive paint and furlike trim.
#RR4 — Leatherette wallet with embossed Roy Rogers figure and all-around zipper closure.
All wallets — Suggested retail . . . $1.00 each
#47 — Elastic suspenders, adjustable to 26" length. Trimmed with detachable badge, metal clips. Individually mounted on display cards. **Suggested retail . . . 69¢**

#RR20 — Satin western tie. Screen painted design. Assorted colors. **Suggested retail . . . 59¢**
#RR12 — Ready-tied boys tie. Assorted colors. **Suggested retail . . . 59¢**
#RR6 — Lariat Tie — Assorted metal slides. 1 doz. on easel-back display. **Suggested retail . . . $1.00**
#RR25 — Satin cowboy tie with metal slide. Screen painted design. Assorted colors. Individually boxed. **Suggested retail . . . 79¢**
#RR11 — Junior boys ready-tied tie. Assorted colors. Sizes: 3-6X. **Suggested retail . . . 59¢**
#RR10 — Colonel tie. Painted design. Assorted colors. 1 doz. on easel-back display card. **Suggested retail . . . 59¢**
#RR30 — Satin square neckerchief. Individually cellophane wrapped. **Suggested retail . . . $1.00**
#0949 — Roy Rogers Robe — Shawl collar, self-yoke, boys wrap robe. Western three-yard cotton flannel print with solid color trim on collar, cuffs, and sash. Sanforized and vat colors. Deputy star badge and Roy Rogers "Golden Book" included in attractive gift box. Sizes: 4-10. Colors: Red print with solid red trim; blue print with solid blue trim; brown print with solid brown trim. **Suggested retail . . . $4.95**

D. H. Neumann Co., Inc.
112 West 34th Street
New York 1, New York

23

1959 – 1960 catalog.

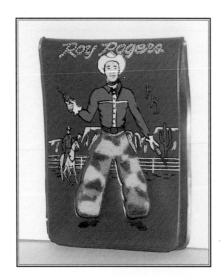

Roy Rogers leather billfold with simulated fur chaps, c. 1950s. C10–$125.00; C8–$75.00; C6–$25.00.

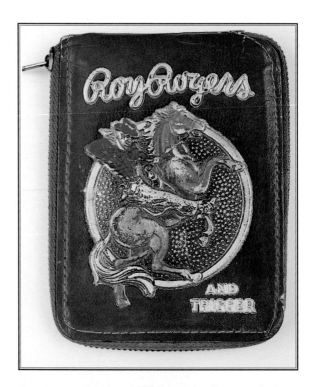

Roy Rogers leather billfold with all-around zipper closure, c.1950s. C10–$125.00; C8–$75.00; C6–$25.00.

Roy Rogers square satin neckerchief, c. 1950s. C10–$75.00; C8–$50.00; C6–$25.00.

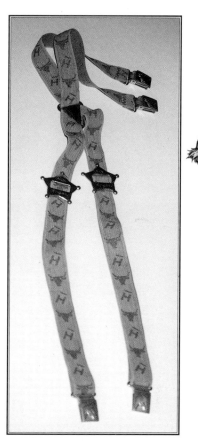

Roy Rogers suspenders, c. 1950s. C10–$125.00; C8–$75.00; C6–$40.00.

Roy Rogers outfit of red shirt with silver metallic decorations and black pants with simulated chaps by J-Bar-T. C10–$200.00; C8–$150.00; C6–$75.00; add $125.00 for original window display box partially shown in photo.

1959 – 1960 catalog.

COLORFUL
AND
WASHABLE

Matching Western Outfits

#922 — Roy Rogers Outfit — Contrasting dark brown and tan cotton twill pants with exclusive colored Roy Rogers stencil design. Shirt is yellow broadcloth with a patterned yoke and suede fringe trim. Extras the cowboy will love are a ribbon and embossed genuine leather belt and holster with gun. Even sizes: 2-12. Individually boxed.
Suggested retail . . . $4.98

#522 — Dale Evans Outfit — The same handsome color combination as above. The cotton twill skirt has colorful Dale Evans stencil design and her full name written in rope. The washable broadcloth shirt has a patterned yoke, suede fringe trim. Sizes: 2-12. Individually boxed.
Suggested retail . . . $4.98

Matching De luxe Suits

#540 — Dale Evans Cowgirl Suit — The beige and brown corduroy skirt and matching vest are elaborately trimmed with eye-catching metal, stars, and DE brand. To complete the outfit, there is a brightly colored washable plaid shirt. Even sizes: 2-12. Individually boxed.
Suggested retail . . . $5.98

#940 — Roy Rogers Cowboy Suit — The same color combination as above — brown and beige corduroy pants with RR brand and a suede belt with lacing, matching vest, and a washable plaid shirt with ribbon tie. The embossed genuine leather belt with holster and gun make this suit a cowpoke's delight. Even sizes: 2-12. Individually boxed.
Suggested retail . . . $5.98

Sackman Bros. Company
200 Fifth Avenue
New York 10, New York

1959 – 60 catalog.

Roy Rogers Official Cowboy Outfit with vest and chaps by Yankiboy, c. 1950s. C10–$200.00; C8–$125.00; C6–$50.00; add $100.00 for original box.

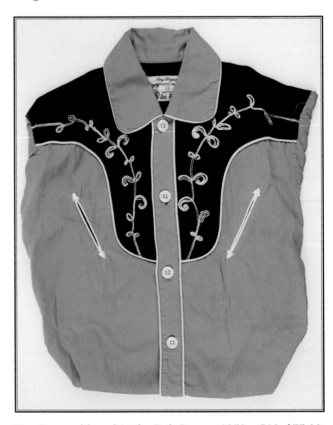

Roy Rogers blue shirt by Rob Roy, c. 1950s. C10–$75.00; C8–$50.00; C6–$25.00.

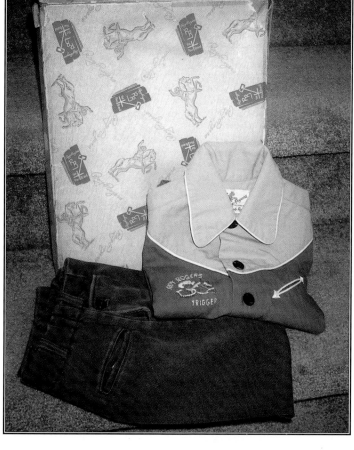

Roy Rogers brown outfit by Rob Roy. C10–$150.00; C8–$75.00; C6–$50.00; add $75.00 for original box.

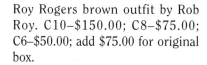

Roy Rogers long sleeve T-shirt, c. 1950s. C10–$75.00; C8–$50.00; C6–$25.00.

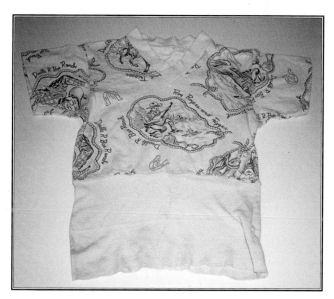

Roy Rogers short sleeve T-shirt with elastic band at waistline, c. 1950s. C10–$75.00; C8–$50.00; C6–$25.00.

143

JACKETS TO FIT ANY OCCASION

Skaggerac Sportswear
Empire State Bldg.
New York 1, New York

"Trail" Leather Jacket
A suede jacket with true western styling — fringed bottom, contrasting cowhide trim on front and back yokes and pockets, and a shining deputy star badge. It is water-repellent for all-weather wear, fully lined, and has a convenient zipper closure.
Colors: Rust, sand, or charcoal.
Suggested retail . . .
Sizes 4-12 . . . **$13.95**
Sizes 14-20 . . . **$16.95**

"Frontier" Leather Jacket
For the young buckaroo who craves that rangeland look at play or dress-up time, this fully fringed suede jacket, adorned by a metal deputy star badge, fills the bill. It is water-repellent and rayon lined throughout for long life and durability.
Colors: Rust, sand, or charcoal.
Suggested retail . . .
Sizes 4-12 . . . **$15.95**
Sizes 14-20 . . . **$19.50**

"Trigger" Cloth Jacket
An ever-popular pioneer-type jacket with plastic fringe on the front and back yokes and bottom, and a deputy star badge. Made of water-repellent wash and wear Bedford Cord, fully nylon lined and has a zipper closure.
Colors: Natural, charcoal, red, taupe, and black.
Suggested retail . . .
Sizes 4-12 . . . **$9.95**
Sizes 14-20 . . . **$12.50**

1959 – 1960 catalog.

Roy Rogers frontier leather jacket (rust color), c. 1950s. C10–$300.00; C8–$150.00; C6–$75.00.

Roy Rogers frontier leather jacket (sand color), c. 1950s. C10–$300.00; C8–$150.00; C6–$75.00.

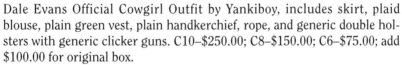

Dale Evans Official Cowgirl Outfit by Yankiboy, includes skirt, plaid blouse, plain green vest, plain handkerchief, rope, and generic double holsters with generic clicker guns. C10–$250.00; C8–$150.00; C6–$75.00; add $100.00 for original box.

Dale Evans Official Cowgirl Outfit by Yankiboy, includes matching skirt and unmarked vest. C10–$200.00; C8–$100.00; C6–$50.00; add $100.00 for original box.

Dale Evans Official Cowgirl Outfit by Yankiboy, includes skirt, vest, hat, and holster. C10–$200.00; C8–$150.00; C6–$75.00; add $100.00 for original box.

Dale Evans cowgirl skirt. C10–$75.00; C8–$50.00; C6–$25.00.

Roy Rogers bunkhouse boots. C10–$125.00;
C8–$75.00; C6–$35.00; add $100.00 for box.

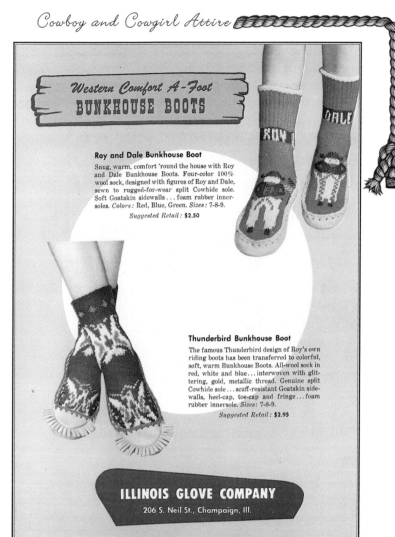

1953 catalog.

Roy Rogers bunkhouse boots box.
C10–$100.00; C8–$50.00; C6–$25.00.

Roy Rogers 9" x 6" boots box. C10–$100.00; C8–$50.00; C6–$25.00.

147

Roy Rogers socks, c. 1950s.
C10–$75.00; C8–$50.00;
C6–$25.00; add $50.00 for
original paper tag.

1959 – 1960 catalog.

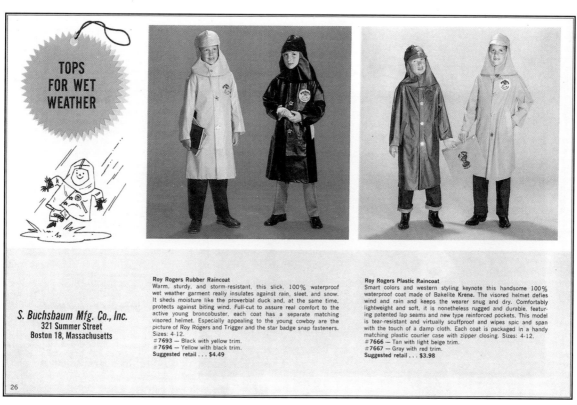

TOPS FOR WET WEATHER

S. Buchsbaum Mfg. Co., Inc.
321 Summer Street
Boston 18, Massachusetts

Roy Rogers Rubber Raincoat
Warm, sturdy, and storm-resistant, this slick, 100% waterproof wet weather garment really insulates against rain, sleet, and snow. It sheds moisture like the proverbial duck and, at the same time, protects against biting wind. Full-cut to assure real comfort to the active young broncobuster, each coat has a separate matching visored helmet. Especially appealing to the young cowboy are the picture of Roy Rogers and Trigger and the star badge snap fasteners. Sizes: 4-12.
#7693 — Black with yellow trim.
#7694 — Yellow with black trim.
Suggested retail . . . $4.49

Roy Rogers Plastic Raincoat
Smart colors and western styling keynote this handsome 100% waterproof coat made of Bakelite Krene. The visored helmet defies wind and rain and keeps the wearer snug and dry. Comfortably lightweight and soft, it is nonetheless rugged and durable, featuring patented lap seams and new type reinforced pockets. This model is tear-resistant and virtually scuffproof and wipes spic and span with the touch of a damp cloth. Each coat is packaged in a handy matching plastic courier case with zipper closing. Sizes: 4-12.
#7666 — Tan with light beige trim.
#7667 — Gray with red trim.
Suggested retail . . . $3.98

26

1959 – 1960 catalog.

Roy Rogers raincoat, all rubber, black with red trim, missing rain cap, c. 1950s. C10–$225.00; C8–$125.00; C6–$75.00.

149

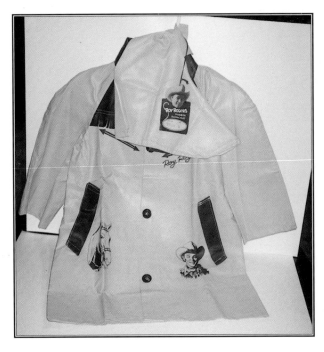

Roy Rogers raincoat and cap, all rubber, yellow with black trim, c. 1950s. Complete C10–$225.00; C8–$150.00; C6–$75.00.

WARMTH
DURABILITY
COMFORT

Illinois Glove Company
602 South Neil Street
Champaign, Illinois

#874 — Suede Cowhide Glove
Fully lined and sueded calf hand. Matching leatherette cuff decorated with picture of Roy and Trigger and deputy star with metal studs and jewels.
Sizes: 4-5-6-7.
Color: Bucktan only.
Suggested retail . . . $1.98
#882C — Capeskin Glove
Fully lined imported capeskin hand. Matching leatherette cuff trimmed with picture of Roy and Trigger and jeweled deputy star. Leather fringe.
Sizes: 5-6-7-8.
Colors: Black and brown.
Suggested retail . . . $2.50

#308C — Capeskin and Suede Gauntlet
Young buckaroos who hanker for a comfortable gauntlet that is tops in rugged wear, warmth, and high western style will find that this item really fills the bill. The hand portion is fully lined and made of fine quality imported capeskin. The handsome garment suede gauntlet is decorated with Roy Rogers' authentic metal signature and Double R Bar Brand. Providing an additional western touch is the leather fringe.
Sizes: 5-6-7-8.
Colors: Black, brown, and cork.
Suggested retail . . . $2.98

LINING IN ALL LEATHER GLOVES GUARANTEED NOT TO PULL OUT

#876 — Two-tone Suede Gauntlet
Fully lined calf hand in russet color. Garment suede cuff is beige with russet fringe and Roy Rogers' signature in gleaming metal for trim.
Sizes: 4-5-6-7.
Color: Two-tone russet and beige only.
Suggested retail . . . $2.50
#666 — Water-repellent Fabric Glove
Fabric is 20% nylon in face. The water-repellent leatherette cuff is decorated with a picture of Roy on Trigger, the Double R Brand, and a deputy star.
Sizes: 4-5-6-7. Colors: #660 Black; #661 Brown; #666 Camel.
Suggested retail . . . 89¢

1959 – 1960 catalog.

Roy Rogers leather gloves with red jewels, c. 1950s. C10–$225.00; C8–$125.00; C6–$50.00.

Roy Rogers leather gloves, c.1950s. C10–$200.00; C8–$100.00; C6–$50.00.
Glove box, one dozen. Box only $125.00.

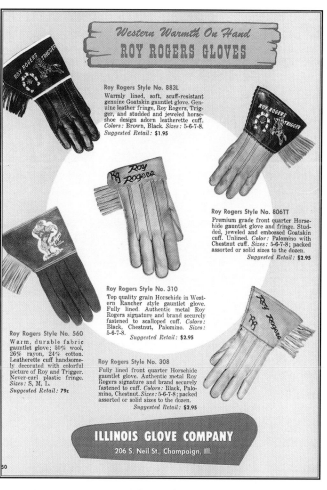

Western Warmth On Hand
ROY ROGERS GLOVES

Roy Rogers Style No. 883L
Warmly lined, soft, scuff-resistant genuine Goatskin gauntlet glove. Genuine leather fringe, Roy Rogers, Trigger, and studded and jeweled horseshoe design adorn leatherette cuff. *Colors:* Brown, Black. *Sizes:* 5-6-7-8. *Suggested Retail:* $1.95

Roy Rogers Style No. 806TT
Premium grade front quarter Horsehide gauntlet glove and fringe. Studded, jeweled and embossed Goatskin cuff. Unlined. *Color:* Palomino with Chestnut cuff. *Sizes:* 5-6-7-8; packed assorted or solid sizes to the dozen. *Suggested Retail:* $2.95

Roy Rogers Style No. 560
Warm, durable fabric gauntlet glove; 50% wool, 26% rayon, 24% cotton. Leatherette cuff handsomely decorated with colorful picture of Roy and Trigger. Never-curl plastic fringe. *Sizes:* S, M, L. *Suggested Retail:* 79¢

Roy Rogers Style No. 310
Top quality grain Horsehide in Western Rancher style gauntlet glove. Fully lined. Authentic metal Roy Rogers signature and brand securely fastened to scalloped cuff. *Colors:* Black, Chestnut, Palomino. *Sizes:* 5-6-7-8. *Suggested Retail:* $2.95

Roy Rogers Style No. 308
Fully lined front quarter Horsehide gauntlet glove. Authentic metal Roy Rogers signature and brand securely fastened to cuff. *Colors:* Black, Palomino, Chestnut. *Sizes:* 5-6-7-8; packed assorted or solid sizes to the dozen. *Suggested Retail:* $2.95

ILLINOIS GLOVE COMPANY
206 S. Neil St., Champaign, Ill.

1953 catalog.

151

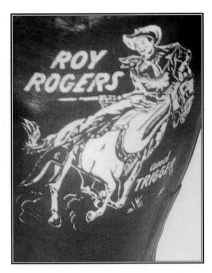

Roy Rogers and Trigger rubber boots, c.1950s.
C10–$300.00; C8–$150.00; C6–$100.00.

Roy Rogers rubber boots, c. 1950s. C10–$300.00; C8–$150.00;
C6-100.00.

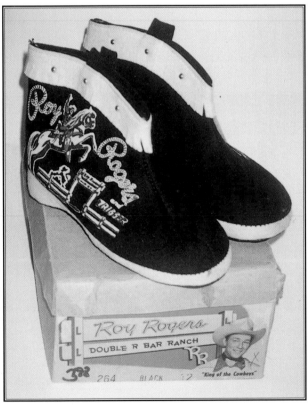

Roy Rogers bedtime boot, c.1950s. C10–$200.00;
C8–$125.00; C6–$75.00; add $125.00 for original box.

1959 – 1960 catalog.

Roy Rogers metal gun and holster tie slide, c. 1950s. C10–$75.00; C8–$50.00; C6–$25.00.

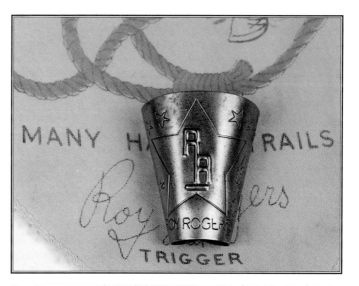

Roy Rogers metal tie slide, c. 1950s. C10–$75.00; C8–$50.00; C6–$25.00.

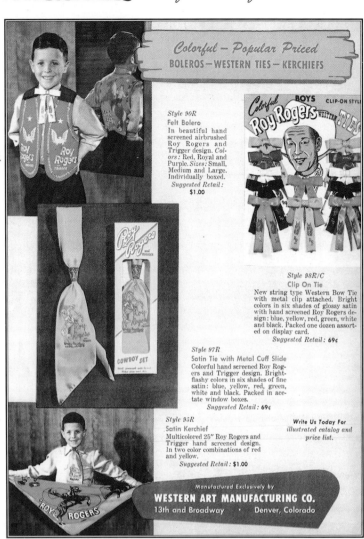

1953 catalog.

Roy Rogers colonel tie, c. 1950s. C10–$125.00; C8–$75.00; C6–$25.00.

Roy Rogers Western Blinkin' Bull bolo tie, c. 1950s. C10–$100.00; C8–$50.00; C6–$25.00; add $100.00 for original backing card.

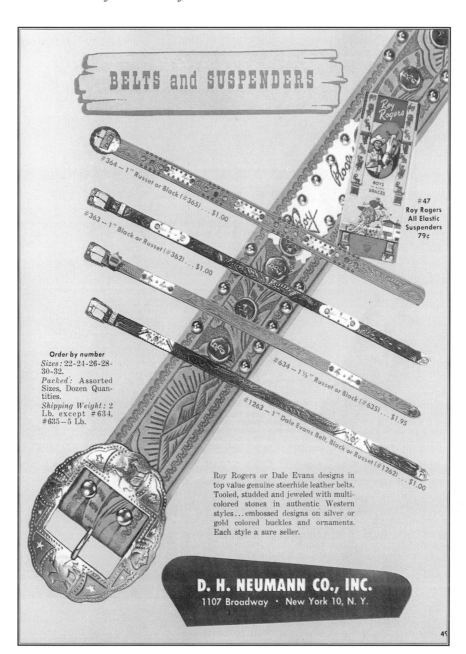

1953 catalog.

Roy Rogers leather belt. C10–$150.00; C8–$75.00; C6–$35.00.

Roy Rogers belt buckle. New item. C10–$35.00.

Roy Rogers leather cuffs, c. 1950s. C10–$200.00; C8–$125.00; C6–$75.00.

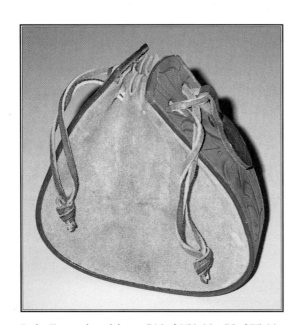

Dale Evans hand bag. C10–$150.00; C8–$75.00; C6–$40.00.

Roy Rogers leather cuffs, c. 1950s. C10–$200.00; C8–$125.00; C6–$75.00.

For Rugged Play
ROY ROGERS JEANS

Roy Rogers
KING OF THE COWBOYS
Frontier "45"

Frontier "45" Western Jeans

Heavy 11 ounce sanforized blue denim with Roy's guns and signature shown on leather tickets on both jeans and jacket. Styling to please every Western minded youngster. Sizes: 4-6-8-10-12.

JEANS — Style #1150 —
Shipping Weight: 14 Lb. per Doz.

Suggested Retail: **$2.79**

JACKET — Style #1151 —
Shipping Weight: 14½ Lb. per Doz.

Suggested Retail: **$2.79**

Roy Rogers
KING OF THE COWBOYS
"DEPUTY SHERIFF"

Deputy Sheriff Western Jeans

Sanforized 8 ounce blue denim Roy Rogers outfit . . . leather Roy Rogers Deputy Sheriff ticket on both jeans and jacket. Designed to take the rough wear given clothes while upholding the law. Sizes: 4-6-8-10-12.

JEANS — Style #850 —
Shipping Weight: 11½ Lb. per Doz.

Suggested Retail: **$1.98**

JACKET — Style #851 —
Shipping Weight: 12 Lb. per Doz.

Suggested Retail: **$1.98**

F.O.B. Virginia

BLUE RIDGE MANUFACTURERS, INC.
350 Fifth Avenue • New York 1, N. Y.

Roy Rogers blue jeans and jacket. 1953 catalog.

Roy Rogers boots. 1959 – 1960 catalog.

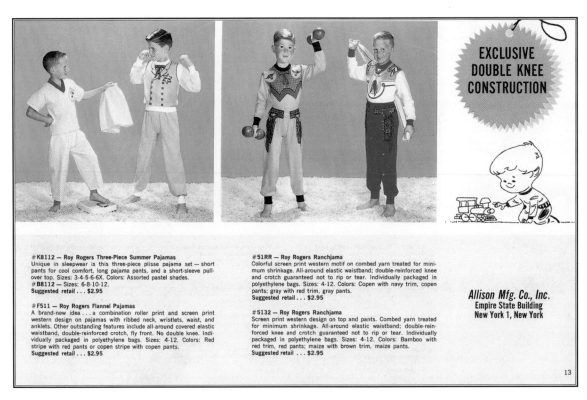

Roy Rogers pajamas. 1959 – 60 catalog.

Guns and Holsters

Parents purchased thousands, if not millions, of Roy Rogers and Dale Evans cap guns and holster sets for their little cowboys and cowgirls in the 50s and early 60s. Classy, Kilgore, Schmidt, Leslie Henry, Buzz Henry, and Hubley all contributed to this hot market during that era. A lot of big cowboys and cowgirls today want that Roy Rogers or Dale Evans gun they had when they were little. The high demand for these guns and holsters has resulted in higher prices for these than for most other Roy Rogers or Dale Evans collectibles. And if you have the box that goes with the gun or holster set you may be looking at a toy cap gun that will bring a much higher price than most real .45 revolvers. Of course there were more little cowboys than cowgirls in the 50s which resulted in fewer Dale Evans guns and holsters produced. Dale Evans guns and holsters will more often than not fetch an even higher price than Roy Rogers guns and holsters. Roy Rogers cast-iron cap guns are the most sought after and will fetch the highest dollar amounts. Unfortunatley no cast-iron guns are depicted in this chapter.

Due the many different variations of holsters not all are depicted in this chapter. Again condition and scarcity are the main factors when trying to determine values of guns and holsters.

Classy Guns

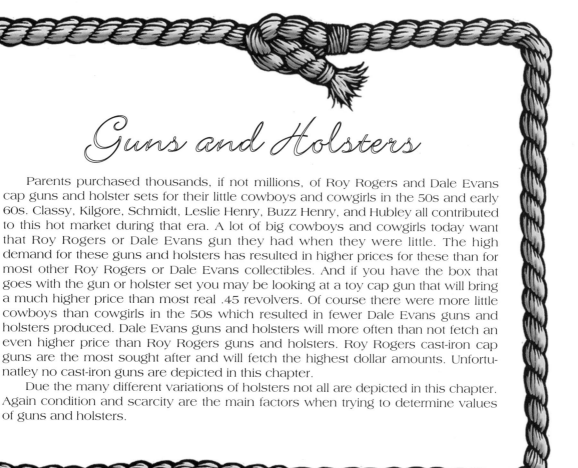

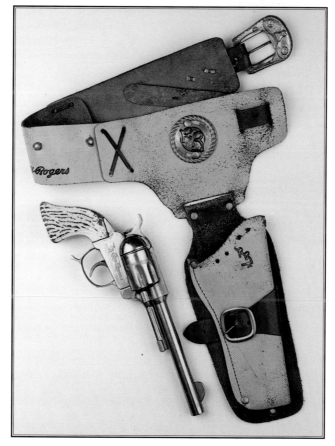

11" die cast with white simulated metal grips, 1955 – 1960 era. C10–$325.00; C8–$200.00; C6–$75.00.

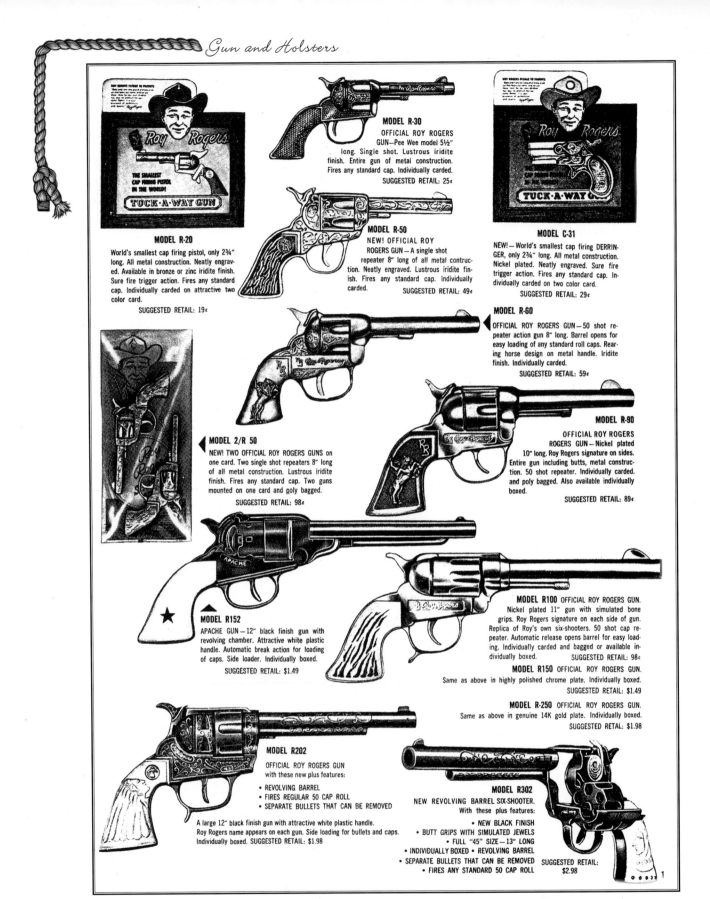

MODEL R-30

OFFICIAL ROY ROGERS GUN—Pee Wee model 5½" long. Single shot. Lustrous iridite finish. Entire gun of metal construction. Fires any standard cap. Individually carded. SUGGESTED RETAIL: 25¢

MODEL R-20

World's smallest cap firing pistol, only 2¾" long. All metal construction. Neatly engraved. Available in bronze or zinc iridite finish. Sure fire trigger action. Fires any standard cap. Individually carded on attractive two color card. SUGGESTED RETAIL: 19¢

MODEL R-50

NEW! OFFICIAL ROY ROGERS GUN—A single shot repeater 8" long of all metal construction. Neatly engraved. Lustrous iridite finish. Fires any standard cap. Individually carded. SUGGESTED RETAIL: 49¢

MODEL C-31

NEW!—World's smallest cap firing DERRINGER, only 2¾" long. All metal construction. Nickel plated. Neatly engraved. Sure fire trigger action. Fires any standard cap. Individually carded on two color card. SUGGESTED RETAIL: 29¢

MODEL R-60

OFFICIAL ROY ROGERS GUN—50 shot repeater action gun 8" long. Barrel opens for easy loading of any standard roll caps. Rearing horse design on metal handle. Iridite finish. Individually carded. SUGGESTED RETAIL: 59¢

MODEL 2/R 50

NEW! TWO OFFICIAL ROY ROGERS GUNS on one card. Two single shot repeaters 8" long of all metal construction. Lustrous iridite finish. Fires any standard cap. Two guns mounted on one card and poly bagged. SUGGESTED RETAIL: 98¢

MODEL R-90

OFFICIAL ROY ROGERS ROGERS GUN—Nickel plated 10" long. Roy Rogers signature on sides. Entire gun including butts, metal construction. 50 shot repeater. Individually carded and poly bagged. Also available individually boxed. SUGGESTED RETAIL: 89¢

MODEL R152

APACHE GUN—12" black finish gun with revolving chamber. Attractive white plastic handle. Automatic break action for loading of caps. Side loader. Individually boxed. SUGGESTED RETAIL: $1.49

MODEL R100 OFFICIAL ROY ROGERS GUN. Nickel plated 11" gun with simulated bone grips. Roy Rogers signature on each side of gun. Replica of Roy's own six-shooters. 50 shot cap repeater. Automatic release opens barrel for easy loading. Individually carded and bagged or available individually boxed. SUGGESTED RETAIL: 98¢

MODEL R150 OFFICIAL ROY ROGERS GUN. Same as above in highly polished chrome plate. Individually boxed. SUGGESTED RETAIL: $1.49

MODEL R-250 OFFICIAL ROY ROGERS GUN. Same as above in genuine 14K gold plate. Individually boxed. SUGGESTED RETAL: $1.98

MODEL R202

OFFICIAL ROY ROGERS GUN with these new plus features:
• REVOLVING BARREL
• FIRES REGULAR 50 CAP ROLL
• SEPARATE BULLETS THAT CAN BE REMOVED

A large 12" black finish gun with attractive white plastic handle. Roy Rogers name appears on each gun. Side loading for bullets and caps. Individually boxed. SUGGESTED RETAIL: $1.98

MODEL R302

NEW REVOLVING BARREL SIX-SHOOTER. With these plus features:
• NEW BLACK FINISH
• BUTT GRIPS WITH SIMULATED JEWELS
• FULL "45" SIZE—13" LONG
• INDIVIDUALLY BOXED • REVOLVING BARREL
• SEPARATE BULLETS THAT CAN BE REMOVED
• FIRES ANY STANDARD 50 CAP ROLL

SUGGESTED RETAIL: $2.98

Catalog page from Classy Gun and Holster Outfits, 1959 – 1960.

11" die-cast nickel finish with gold finished scroll grips, 1955 – 1960 era. C10–$350.00; C8–$225.00; C6–$100.00.

9½" nickel-plated 50 shot repeater Model R90, all metal constructed. C10–$200.00; C8–$125.00; C6–$75.00.

8" nickel-plated cap gun with engraving, Model R60.   C10–$300.00; C8–$225.00; C6–$100.00.

2¾" bronze cap pistol with miniature holster, c. 1950. C10–$75.00; C8–$40.00; C6–$20.00; add $25.00 for holster.
Roy Rogers five-star deputy badge, c. 1950. C10–$35.00; C8–$25.00; C6–$15.00.

2¾" zinc finish carded cap gun, c. 1950s. C10–$75.00; C8–$40.00; C6–$20.00; add $75.00 for backing card.

Four different color variations of 11" cap guns. C10–$350.00 – $500.00 each

Classy guns from 1950 – 1960 catalog.

Kilgore Guns

9" nickel die cast with long ejector rod with tan chocolate swirl horsehead grips, 1955. C10 $200.00; C8–$125.00; C6–$50.00, add $125.00; for original rack card.

Shootin' Iron, rare, large 10½" nickel finish with six shot revolving cylinder, c. 1955 – 60. C10–$400.00; C8–$250.00; C6–$100.00; add $350.00 for original box.

8" nickel die cast with short ejector rod with violet, brown, and white swirl grips, 1955. C10–$175.00; C8–$100.00; C6–$50.00.

Same as above with restored gold finish. To my knowledge was never produced with gold finish. Restored–$100.00.

20" x 16" gun display, rare, 1950 – 1955. C10–$600.00; C8–$350.00; C6–$150.00.

Leslie Henry Guns

9" high hammer with polished nickel finish, also produced in rare gold finish with black grips.
Nickel finish, C10–$300.00; C8–$225.00; C6–$100.00.
Gold finish, C10–$400.00; C8–$300.00; C6–$150.00 (not shown).

George Schmidt Cap Guns

9¾" nickel plated with long ribbed barrel, fully engraved frame with RR engraved checkered copper grips, 1950 – 1960 era, also came with red jewels. C10–$400.00; C8–$225.00; C6–$100.00; add $25.00 – 50.00 for jewels; add $300.00 for original box.

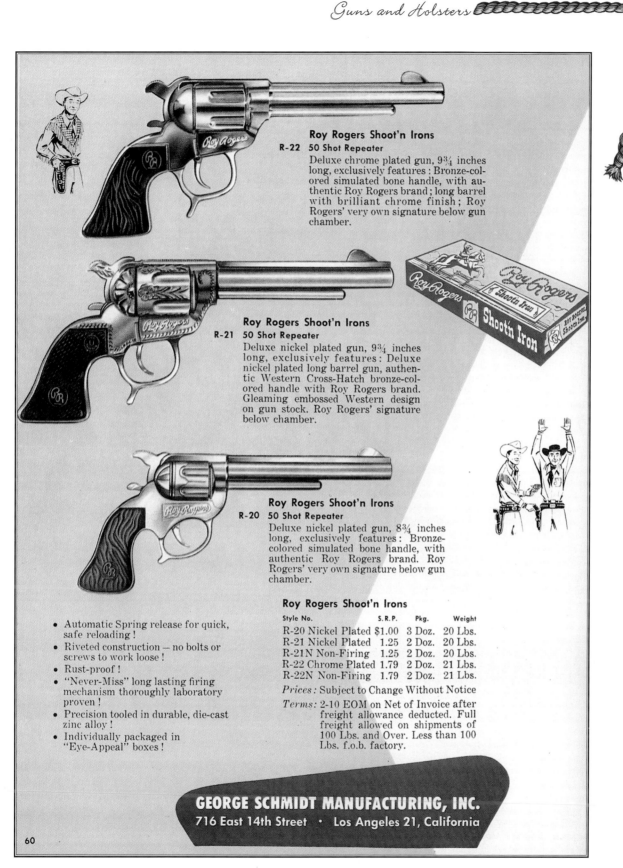

Roy Rogers Shoot'n Irons

R-22 50 Shot Repeater

Deluxe chrome plated gun, 9¾ inches long, exclusively features : Bronze-colored simulated bone handle, with authentic Roy Rogers brand ; long barrel with brilliant chrome finish ; Roy Rogers' very own signature below gun chamber.

Roy Rogers Shoot'n Irons

R-21 50 Shot Repeater

Deluxe nickel plated gun, 9¾ inches long, exclusively features : Deluxe nickel plated long barrel gun, authentic Western Cross-Hatch bronze-colored handle with Roy Rogers brand. Gleaming embossed Western design on gun stock. Roy Rogers' signature below chamber.

Roy Rogers Shoot'n Irons

R-20 50 Shot Repeater

Deluxe nickel plated gun, 8¾ inches long, exclusively features : Bronze-colored simulated bone handle, with authentic Roy Rogers brand. Roy Rogers' very own signature below gun chamber.

Roy Rogers Shoot'n Irons

Style No.		S.R.P.	Pkg.	Weight
R-20	Nickel Plated	$1.00	3 Doz.	20 Lbs.
R-21	Nickel Plated	1.25	2 Doz.	20 Lbs.
R-21N	Non-Firing	1.25	2 Doz.	20 Lbs.
R-22	Chrome Plated	1.79	2 Doz.	21 Lbs.
R-22N	Non-Firing	1.79	2 Doz.	21 Lbs.

Prices : Subject to Change Without Notice

Terms : 2-10 EOM on Net of Invoice after freight allowance deducted. Full freight allowed on shipments of 100 Lbs. and Over. Less than 100 Lbs. f.o.b. factory.

- Automatic Spring release for quick, safe reloading !
- Riveted construction — no bolts or screws to work loose !
- Rust-proof !
- "Never-Miss" long lasting firing mechanism thoroughly laboratory proven !
- Precision tooled in durable, die-cast zinc alloy !
- Individually packaged in "Eye-Appeal" boxes !

GEORGE SCHMIDT MANUFACTURING, INC.
716 East 14th Street • Los Angeles 21, California

60

1953 Roy Rogers/Dale Evans Catalogue and Merchants Manual.

Same gun as on page 166 with cap firing hammer (top) and non-firing hammer (right). Add $100.00; for non-firing hammer.

Same gun with box as on page 166 (left). Similar 9¾" gun with highly polished chrome plated, came with checkered or simulated bone copper grips, c. 1950 – 1960. C10–$275.00; C8–$175.00; C6–$100.00; add $300.00 for box. (See illustration at top of page 167.)

8¾" nickel plated with checkered copper RR grips, top with blue jewel, bottom with yellow stone, also came with red and green stones, rare. C10–$500.00; C8–$350.00; C6–$150.00.

8¾" smaller nickel-plated framed version gun with copper simulated bone copper grips, rare, 1950 – 1960. C10–$300.00; C8–$175.00; C6–$100.00; add $300.00 for original box.

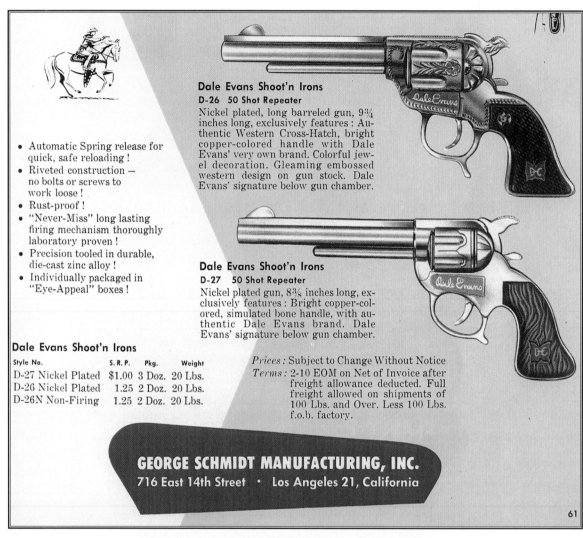

- Automatic Spring release for quick, safe reloading!
- Riveted construction — no bolts or screws to work loose!
- Rust-proof!
- "Never-Miss" long lasting firing mechanism thoroughly laboratory proven!
- Precision tooled in durable, die-cast zinc alloy!
- Individually packaged in "Eye-Appeal" boxes!

Dale Evans Shoot'n Irons
D-26 50 Shot Repeater
Nickel plated, long barreled gun, 9¾ inches long, exclusively features: Authentic Western Cross-Hatch, bright copper-colored handle with Dale Evans' very own brand. Colorful jewel decoration. Gleaming embossed western design on gun stock. Dale Evans' signature below gun chamber.

Dale Evans Shoot'n Irons
D-27 50 Shot Repeater
Nickel plated gun, 8¾ inches long, exclusively features: Bright copper-colored, simulated bone handle, with authentic Dale Evans brand. Dale Evans' signature below gun chamber.

Dale Evans Shoot'n Irons

Style No.	S.R.P.	Pkg.	Weight
D-27 Nickel Plated	$1.00	3 Doz.	20 Lbs.
D-26 Nickel Plated	1.25	2 Doz.	20 Lbs.
D-26N Non-Firing	1.25	2 Doz.	20 Lbs.

Prices: Subject to Change Without Notice
Terms: 2-10 EOM on Net of Invoice after freight allowance deducted. Full freight allowed on shipments of 100 Lbs. and Over. Less 100 Lbs. f.o.b. factory.

GEORGE SCHMIDT MANUFACTURING, INC.
716 East 14th Street • Los Angeles 21, California

61

Dale Evans 9¾" nickel plated, ribbed barrel with butterfly grips and red jewels, rare. C10–$500.00; C8–$350.00; C6–$150.00
Dale Evans 8¾" smaller nickel-plated framed version, rare. C10–$425.00; C8–$300.00; C6–$125.00.
1953 catalog.

Buzz Henry

Dale Evans 7½", rare gold finish with black grips, c. 1950 – 1955.
C10–$500.00; C8–$300.00; C6–$100.00.

Stevens

Trigger, 7½" die-cast repeaters with cowboy and crossed grips. C10–$150.00;
C8–$100.00; C6–$50.00 each.

Louis Marx Cap Rifles

Roy Rogers 35" brown plastic and metal
Winchester Deluxe Model 71, c. 1950s.
C10–$350.00; C8–$225.00; C6–$125.00.

1959 – 60 catalog.

Roy Rogers 25" silver plastic and metal
Deluxe Winchester with crosshatched
grips, c. 1950s. C10–$300.00;
C8–$150.00; C6–$75.00; add $250.00 for
box (not shown).

Holsters and Gun Sets

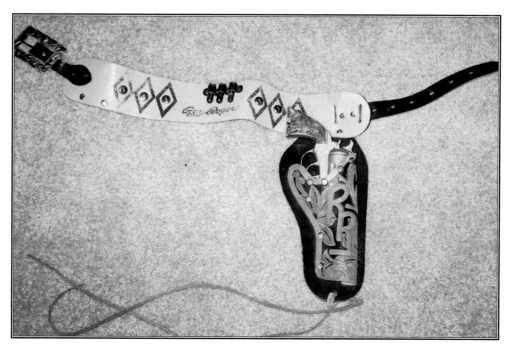

Roy Rogers single leather holster, shown with Kilgore cap gun. Holster only, c. 1950s, C10–$200.00; C8–$125.00; C6–$50.00.

Roy Rogers single red and white simulated holster with plain belt, c. 1950s. C10–$100.00; C8–$65.00; C6–$30.00.

Roy Rogers single white and silver metallic holster, c. 1950s. C10–$200.00; C8–$125.00; C6–$75.00.

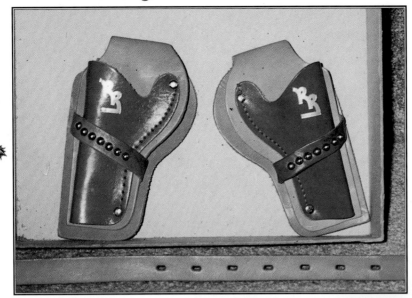

Boxed Classy holster set, possibly for the 5" Model R30 single shot. Holsters and box only, c. 1950s. C10–$500.00; C8–$350.00; C6–$100.00.

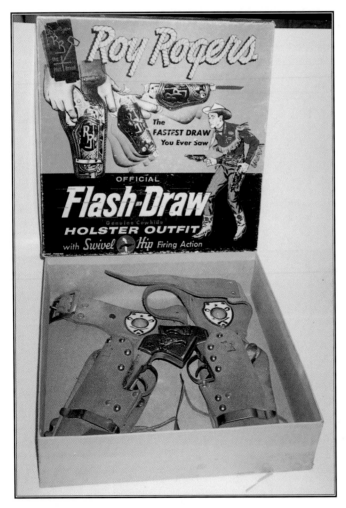

Roy Rogers Flash Draw double holster outfit with turquoise stones with pair of Classy metal rearing horse grip guns, c. 1950s. Complete set, C10–$1,500.00; C8–$750.00; C6–$300.00.

174

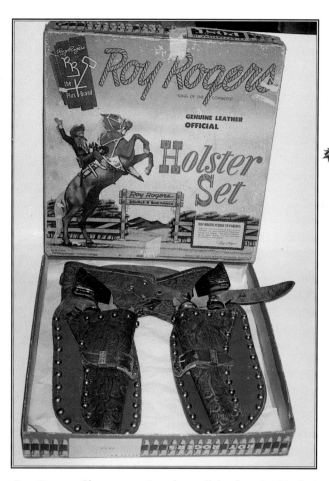

Roy Rogers Classy two-piece box, all leather double holsters with Classy guns, c. 1950s. Complete, C10–$1,500.00, C8–$1,000.00, C6–$400.00.

Roy Rogers Classy two-piece box, all leather holsters with Classy guns, c. 1950s. Complete, C10–$1,500.00, C8–$1,000.00, C6–$400.00.

Roy Rogers Classy boxed holster set with black and brown tooled leather holsters with silver metallic strips with Roy Rogers inscription at top of belt, c. 1950s. C10–$750.00, C8–$450.00, C6–$250.00.

Roy Rogers Classy boxed brown leather holsters with pair of Classy guns, c. 1950s. Complete, C10–$1,500.00, C8–$1,000.00, C6–$400.00.

Roy Rogers small brown leather holsters with silver and gold conchos, shown with Kilgore guns, c. 1950s. Holsters only, C10–$350.00; C8–$150.00; C6–$65.00.

Roy Rogers brown simulated leather and silver metallic inscribed holsters with red jewels. C10–$175.00; C8–$100.00; C6–$50.00.

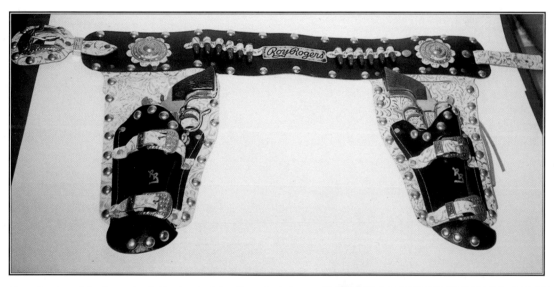

Roy Rogers black and white tooled leather holsters, shown with Classy guns. Holsters only, C10–$500.00; C8–$300.00; C6–$150.00.

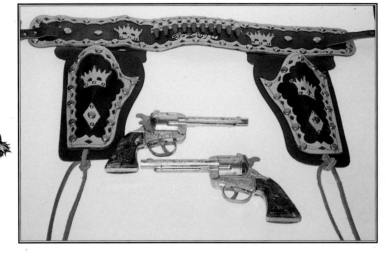

Roy Rogers dark brown and tan holsters with large metal belt buckle, c. 1950s. Holster only, C10–$450.00; C8–$250.00; C6–$125.00.

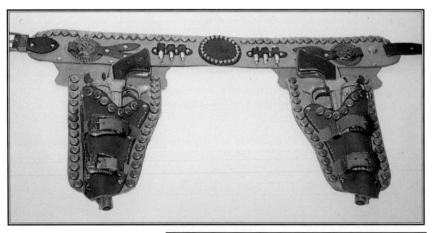

Roy Rogers tan and brown holsters with numerous metal buttons, shown with G. Schmidt guns, c. 1950s. Holsters only, C10–$500.00; C8–$300.00; C6–$150.00.

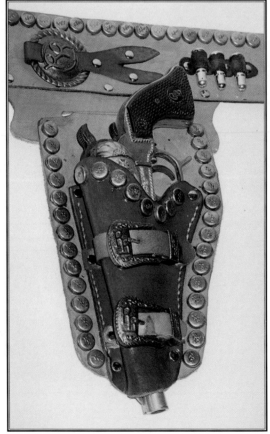

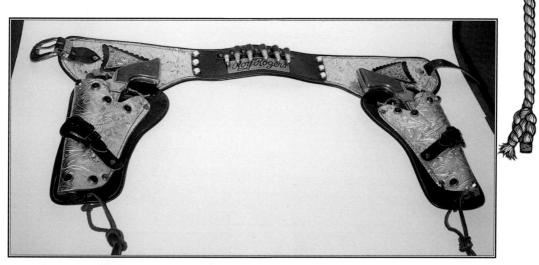

Roy Rogers dark brown and metallic gold holsters with brown stones, shown with Schmidt guns, c. 1950s. Holsters only, C10–$550.00; C8–$325.00; C6–$175.00.

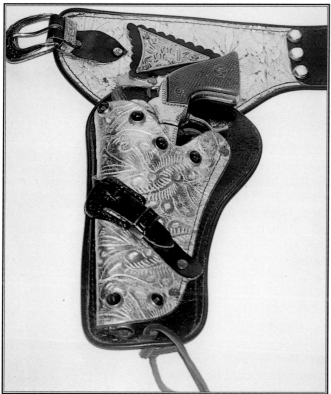

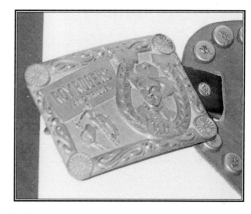

Roy Rogers brown and black tooled leather holsters with red stones with large metal belt buckle, shown with Schmidt guns, c. 1950s. Holsters only, C10–$450.00; C8–$250.00; C6–$125.00.

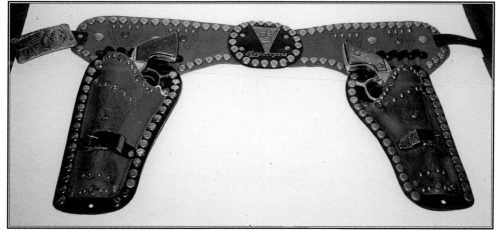

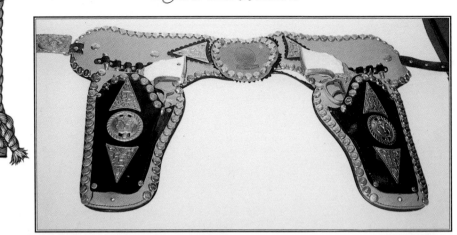

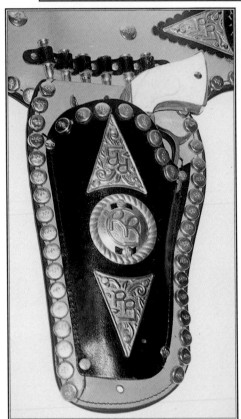

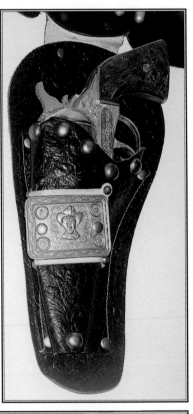

Roy Rogers black and tanned tooled leather holsters with metal conchos and triangular metal conchos with Roy Rogers inscribed. Holsters only, C10–$500.00; C8–$300.00; C6–$150.00.

Roy Rogers black tooled leather holsters with rectangular metal conchos with Roy Rogers's name and profile inscribed, shown with Kilgore guns. Holsters only, C10–$400.00; C8–$200.00; C6–$100.00.

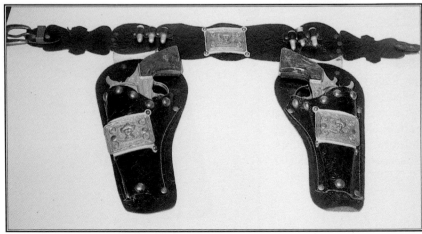

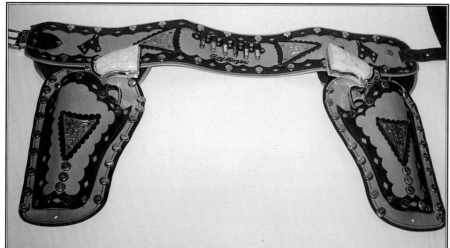

Roy Rogers brown and tan simulated leather holsters with triangular conchos with inscription, shown with Kilgore guns. Holsters only, C10–$450.00; C8–$250.00; C6–$125.00.

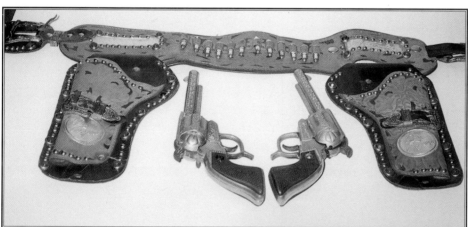

Roy Rogers brown and black simulated leather holsters with circular conchos with Roy Rogers inscription, shown with Schmidt guns, c. 1950s. Holsters only, C10–$425.00; C8–$225.00; C6–$125.00.

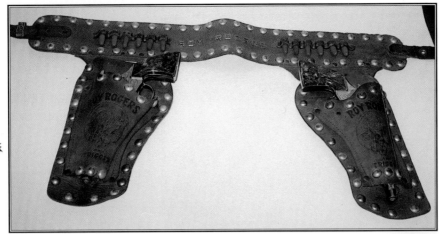

Brown leather holsters with Roy Rogers's name on belt with metal letters, shown with Kilgore guns. Holsters only, C10–$350.00; C8–$150.00; C6–$75.00.

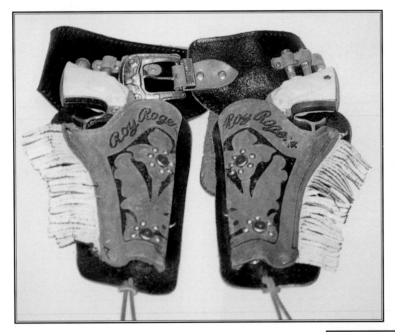

Roy Rogers brown and black tooled leather holsters with flower design with red jewels, shown with Kilgore guns, c. 1950s. Holsters only, C10–$300.00; C8–$150.00; C6–$75.00.

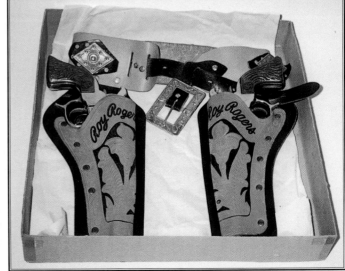

Roy Rogers holsters, same as above with no jewels and different belt buckle, shown with Classy guns, c. 1950s. Holster only, C10–$300.00; C8–$150.00; C6–$75.00.

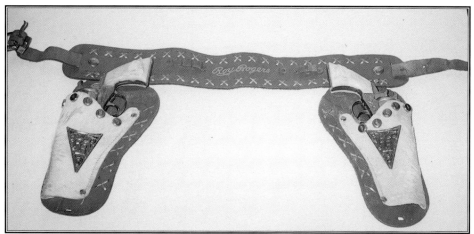

Roy Rogers brown and cream simulated leather holsters with triangular metal conchos, shown with Kilgore guns. Holsters only, C10–$400.00; C8–$200.00; C6–$100.00.

Brown and tan fringed holsters with Roy Rogers's name inscribed on belt, shown with Kilgore guns. Holsters only, C10–$250.00; C8–$125.00; C6–$75.00.

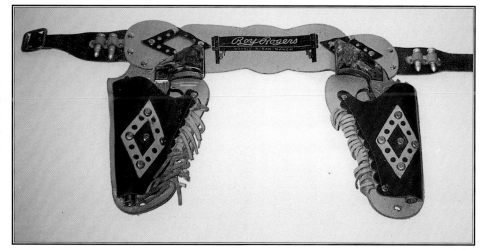

183

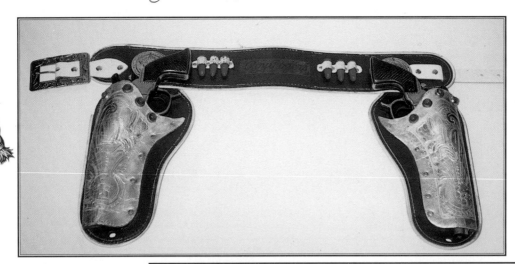

Roy Rogers brown with gold metallic holsters with inscription, shown with Schmidt guns, c. 1950s. Holsters only, C10–$300.00; C8–$150.00; C6–$75.00.

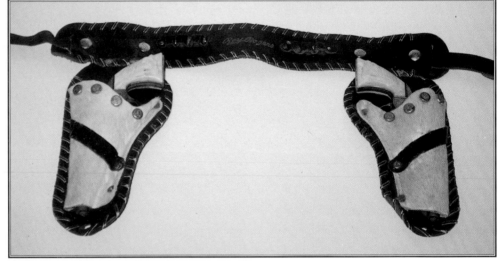

Roy Rogers black and cream holsters with inscription on belt, shown with Kilgore guns, c. 1950s. Holster only, C10–$250.00; C8–$125.00; C6–$75.00.

Roy Rogers brown simulated leather holsters (fast draw), shown with Classy guns. Holsters only, C10–$300.00; C8–$150.00; C6–$75.00.

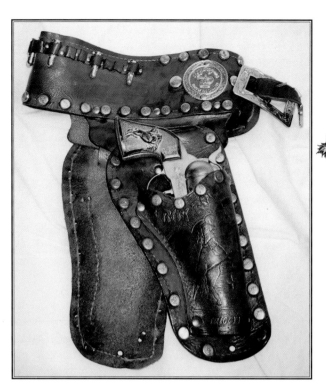

Roy Rogers brown and black simulated leather holsters with large RR inscribed, c. 1950s. C10–$175.00; C8–$100.00; C6–$50.00.

Tooled leather holsters with crown conchos on belt, with Roy Rogers and rearing Trigger on holsters, shown with Classy Guns, c. 1950s. Holsters only, C10–$325.00; C8–$150.00; C6–$75.00.

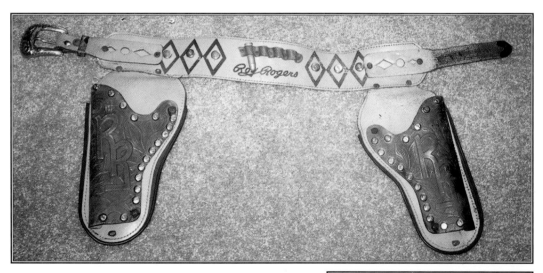

Roy Rogers brown and tan simulated leather holsters with large RR engraved. C10–$250.00; C8–$125.00; C6–$60.00.

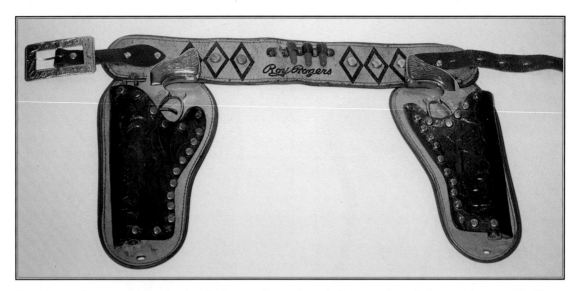

Roy Rogers brown and tan leather holsters, almost identical to previous holsters, shown with Classy guns, c. 1950s. Holsters only, C10–$250.00; C8–$125.00; C6–$60.00.

Roy Rogers Classy Fast Draw holster, shown with Kilgore gun.
Holster only, C10–$200.00; C8–$100.00; C6–$50.00.

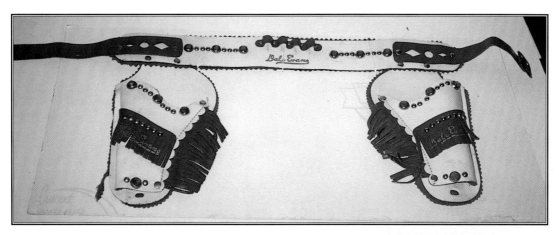

Dale Evans red and white fringed double holsters with red jewels, c. 1950s. C10–$400.00; C8–$200.00; C6–$100.00.

Classy Roy Rogers clover leaf spurs. C10–$250.00; C8–$125.00; C6–$75.00; add $200.00 for box.

Roy Rogers Classy gold star spurs with metal crown concho. C10–$150.00; C8- $100.00; C6–$50.00; add $200.00 for box.

Roy Rogers Classy silver star spurs. C10–$150.00; C8–$100.00; C6–$50.00; add $200.00 for box.

Roy Rogers Spurs

R-30 Chrome finish with bronze trim. Genuine leather straps with Roy Rogers brand on chrome plated concha.

Roy Rogers Spurs

R-31 Nickel plated finish with Roy Rogers brand on nickel plated concha. Genuine leather straps.

Roy Rogers Spurs

R-36 Nickel plated finish. Genuine leather straps with authentic Roy Rogers signature.

Style No.	S.R.P.	Pkg.	Weight
R-36 Nickel Plated	$1.19	2 Doz.	14 Lbs.
R-31 Nickel Plated w/Concha	1.49	2 Doz.	17 Lbs.
R-30 Chrome Plated w/Concha	1.98	2 Doz.	18 Lbs.

Prices: Subject to Change Without Notice

Terms: 2-10 EOM on Net of Invoice after Freight Allowance deducted. Full Freight allowed on shipments of 100 Lbs. f.o.b. factory.

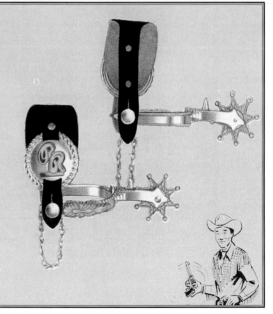

George Schmidt Spurs, 1959 – 1960 catalog.

Miscellaneous Toys

Due to Roy's success, starring in 85 westerns and then "The Roy Rogers Show" from 1951 to 1957, sponsors and toy companies clamored to get Roy's and Dale's name on their product. Sales boomed, and there were hundreds if not thousands of great toys produced. Many collectors today are looking for that rare or unusual toy that no one has ever heard of or seen. Due to the many toys produced with Roy's and Dale's endorsement, it is certain that there are many toys not listed in this chapter.

Again condition and scarcity dictate the value. I can't over emphasize the importance of the original box. Boxes or original packaging can easily in most cases double the value.

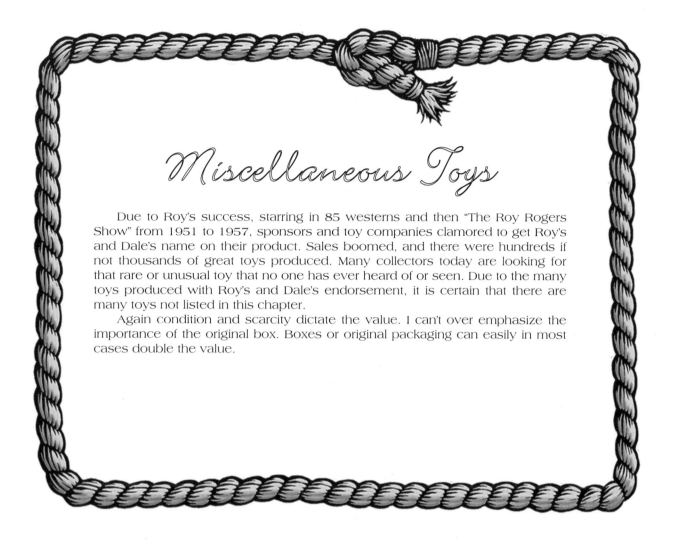

Roy Rogers Marx stagecoach wagon train, red version, 2" x 2" x 14", long plastic and tin wind-up train, c. 1950s. C10–$300.00; C8–$200.00; C6–$75.00; add $200.00 for box.

Roy Rogers Marx stagecoach wagon train, blue version, same as red, blue being rarer, c. 1950s. C10–$350.00; C8–$250.00; C6–$100.00; add $200.00; for box.

Roy Rogers & Trigger, wall savings lithographed tin bank by Ohio Art Co., 8" x 6", c. 1950s. C10–$250.00; C8–$150.00; C6–$75.00; add $50.00 for original lock and key; add $100.00 for original packaging.

Band Set by Spec-Toy-Celars, Inc., box measures 17½" x 14½" x 3", c. 1953. C10–$400.00; C8–$225.00; C6–$75.00. Toys are not marked Roy Rogers.

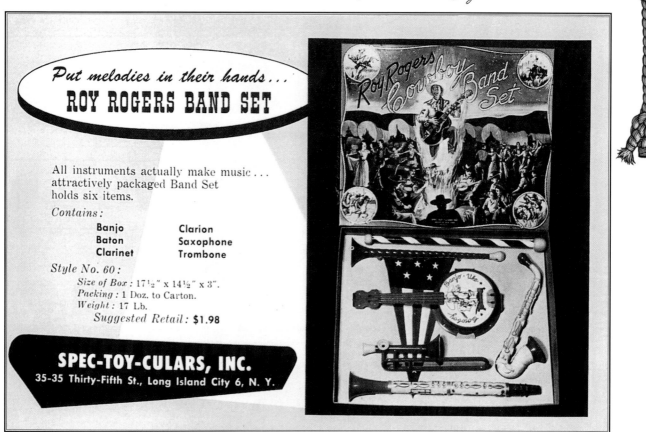

Put melodies in their hands...

ROY ROGERS BAND SET

All instruments actually make music...
attractively packaged Band Set
holds six items.

Contains:

Banjo	**Clarion**
Baton	**Saxophone**
Clarinet	**Trombone**

Style No. 60:
  Size of Box : 17½" x 14½" x 3".
  Packing : 1 Doz. to Carton.
  Weight : 17 Lb.
    Suggested Retail: $1.98

SPEC-TOY-CULARS, INC.
35-35 Thirty-Fifth St., Long Island City 6, N. Y.

1953 catalog.

Roy Rogers 8½" battery operated ranch lantern by Ohio
Art Co., c. 1950s. C10–$200.00; C8–$100.00; C6–$50.00;
add $250.00 for box.

Nellybelle Jeep with Roy, Dale, and Bullet figures, by Marx, made of pressed steel, measures approx. 5" x 5" x 11", c. 1950s. C10–$500.00; C8–$350.00; C6–$200.00; add $300.00 for box.

Metal hauler and van trailer with plastic Nellybelle Jeep and plastic figures, by Marx, truck measures approx. 11" long, c. 1950s. C10–$400.00; C8–$200.00; C6–$100.00; add $300.00 for box.

Camera with telescopic sight by Herbert George Co., approx. 3½" x 3½" x 4", c. 1950s. C10–$200.00; C8–$100.00; C6–$50.00; add $100.00 for box.

Camera with flash attachment, by Herbert George Co., c. 1950s. C10–$175.00; C8–$85.00; C6–$35.00; add $100.00 for box.

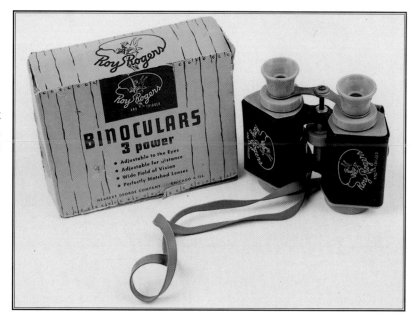

Three-power binoculars, by Herbert George Co., approx. 4½" x 4", c. 1950s. C10–$150.00; C8–$75.00; C6–$40.00; add $100.00 for box.

Sells on Sight
CAMERAS AND BINOCULARS

**5-Power 2-Section
All Aluminum Telescope**

2-section, scientifically and durably constructed telescope with 5-power, optically ground and pitch-polished lenses. Extra wide field of vision. Designed to deflect light. 7⅜ in. closed, 10½ in. extended. *Suggested Retail :* **$1.29**

Packed : 72 in carton. *Shipping Weight :* 15 Lb.

6-Power 3-Section All Aluminum Telescope

A powerful telescope with as much sales appeal to adults as to youngsters! Sturdily and scientifically made. Optically ground and polished lenses.

Suggested Retail : **$1.98**

Roy Rogers Flash Camera

Features : Flash attachment snaps on and off in a second – ejector for used bulbs. Takes 12 2¼″ x 2¼″ pictures on a 620 roll. Highly ground and polished lens. Shutter speed of approximately 1/50 second. Telescopic sight. Unbreakable plastic, metal trim. Guaranteed.

Suggested Retail : **$4.49** *tax paid*
Packed : 24 in carton
Shipping Weight : 30 Lb.

Roy Rogers Camera

Same as the above, without Flash unit.
Suggested Retail : **$3.49** *tax paid*
Packed : 48 in carton.
Shipping Weight : 31 Lb.

Roy Rogers Flash Camera Photographic Kit

Compact, Graceful, Popular Box Type Camera ...with telescopic view finder lenses. Handy carrying strap. Takes 12 2¼″ x 2¼″ clear pictures. Also beautiful color pictures. Flash attachment snaps on and off easily...ejects hot bulbs. Complete with everything needed to take flash pictures. Handsome Photographic Gadget Bag with two zippers and carrying strap. Handsome display package.

Suggested Retail : **$9.95** *tax paid*

Roy Rogers 3-Power Binoculars

Adjustable for focal length. Adjustable for eye separation. Genuine American Optical lenses – perfectly matched, ground and pitch-polished. Complete with simulated leather shoulder strap. Recessed eye lenses to eliminate light and reflections. Styled to fit hands comfortably. Wide field of vision. Black leatherette finish with taupe plastic and polished metal trim.

Simulated Leather Carrying Case : **59c**

Suggested Retail : **$2.98**
Packed : 36 in carton. *Shipping Weight :* 21 Lb.

**Roy Rogers Official
Flash Camera and Binocular Set**

With Roll of Ansco 620 film. Packaged in attractive gift box.

Suggested Retail : **$7.98** *tax paid*

HERBERT GEORGE COMPANY
311 N. Desplaines St. • Chicago 6, Ill.

76

1953 catalog.

Wood Burning Set, c. 1950s.
C10–$300.00; C8–$175.00;
C6–$75.00.

Horseshoe Set by Ohio Art Co., contents two tin litho 6" dia. disks, two black, two red rubber horseshoes with Roy and Trigger inscription, and two metal screw-on pegs, c. 1950s. C10–$150.00; C8–$100.00; C6–$50.00. Add $100.00 for box.

Horseshoe set by Ohio Art Co., same as previous set, except in plastic carded bag, c. 1950s. Add $75.00 for original bag package.

Horseshoe set by Ohio Art Co., 8" dia. tin litho disc, c. 1950s. C10–$175.00; C8–$125.00; C6–$75.00; add $125.00 for box.

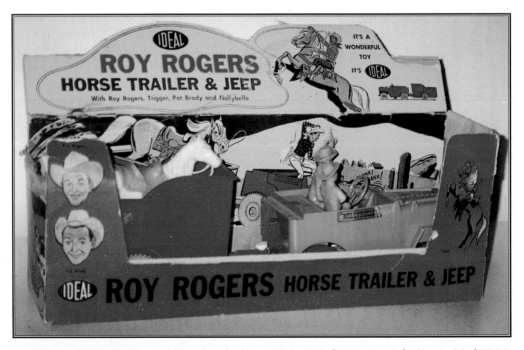

Roy Rogers Horse Trailer and Jeep by Ideal, c. 1950s. C10–$250.00; C8–$150.00; C6–$75.00; add $150.00 for box.

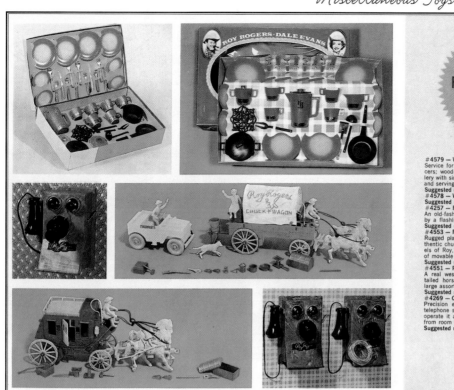

#4579 — Western Dinner Set
Service for four. Colorful metal plates and saucers; wood-grained plastic cups; aluminum cutlery with simulated wood handles; all the cooking and serving pieces a cowboy or girl will need.
Suggested retail. . . $5.00
#4578 — Western Dinner Set (Service for two)
Suggested retail . . . $3.00
#4257 — Roy Rogers Western Telephone
An old-fashioned telephone of plastic. Operated by a flashlight battery, it actually rings.
Suggested retail . . . $3.00
#4553 — Roy Rogers Chuck Wagon and Jeep
Rugged plastic models of Nellybelle and an authentic chuck wagon, complete with lifelike models of Roy, Dale, Pat Brady, and Bullet. Scores of movable parts and miniature tools.
Suggested retail . . . $6.00
#4551 — Roy Rogers Stagecoach
A real western stagecoach, two beautifully detailed horses which can be unhitched, and a large assortment of extra pieces for fix-it fun.
Suggested retail . . . $4.00
#4269 — Communicating Telephone Set
Precision engineered authentic plastic western telephone set with all the equipment needed to operate it and ring the bells. Carries messages from room to room or house to house.
Suggested retail . . . $10.00

Ideal Toy Corp.
200 Fifth Ave.
New York 10, N.Y.

1959–1960 catalog.

Roy Rogers Fix-It Stage Coach by Ideal, approx. 5" x 6" x 15", plastic, c. 1955. There were two drivers one was Roy Rogers and the other the bearded stagecoach driver. C10–$200.00; C8–$100.00; C6–$65.00; add $125.00 for box.

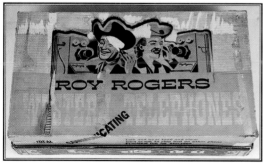

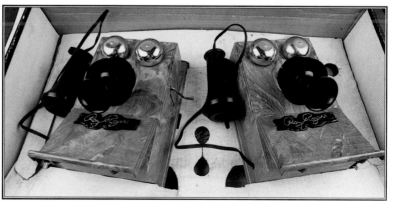

Roy Rogers Double Western Telephone Set by Ideal with Roy and Dale on front of box. C10–$200.00; C8–$125.00; C6–$75.00; add $200.00 for box.

Roy Rogers Single Western Telephone by Ideal with Roy on front of box, c. 1950s. C10–$150.00; C8–$75.00; C6–$30.00; add $150.00; for box.

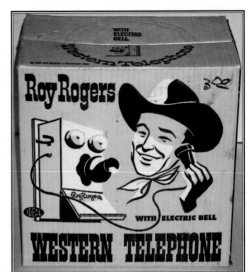

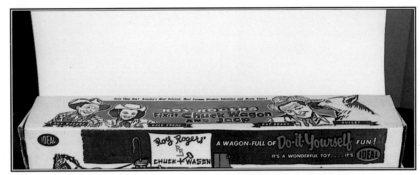

Roy Rogers Fix-It Chuck Wagon and Jeep by Ideal, approx. 4½" x 7" x 24", more than 60 different parts, c. 1950s. C10–$225.00; C8–$125.00; C6–$75.00; add $125.00 for box.

Western Dinner Set for two by Ideal, c. 1950s. C10–$150.00; C8–$100.00; C6–$50.00; add $150.00 for box.

Western Dinner Set for four by Ideal, c. 1950s. C10–$250.00; C8–$150.00; C6–$75.00; add $150.00 for box.

Roy Rogers Quick Shooter, contains black felt hat with pop out Derringer miniature cap pistol by Ideal, c. 1950s. C10–$200.00; C8–$150.00; C6–$75.00; add $200.00 for box.

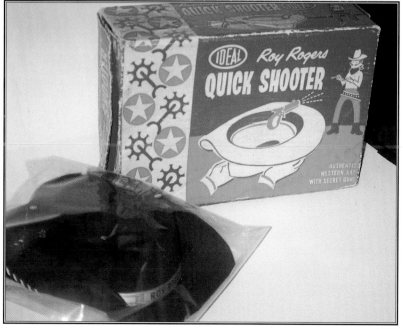

Roy Rogers Riders Harmonica No. 300-R

Here's something new that the kids will really go for. This electronically tuned instrument has 10 holes, 20 plastic reeds that give a true soft tone quality and metal instrument resonance. The metal covers, handsomely engraved with Roy Rogers' name and good luck horseshoe, are a sure-fire appeal to all kids. This low priced best seller is packaged in a colorful individual box with Roy Rogers' picture on two sides. Each is cellophane wrapped with instruction folder.

Suggested Retail: 60c

HARMONIC REED CORPORATION
1111 W. Lancaster Ave., Rosemont, Pa.

Roy Rogers Cowboy Band Harmonica No. 350-R

This is real value! A precision tuned harmonica with ten solid brass reeds on each of two brass plates. Engraved metal covers. This "King of the Cowboys" harmonica is a real eye-catcher and has great appeal to children of all ages. Individually packaged in a smart box with Roy Rogers' picture and autograph. Each is cellophane wrapped with an instruction folder.

Suggested Retail: $1.00

1953 catalog.

Roy Rogers Riders Harmonica by Reed Harmonica Division, in original blister pack C10–$75.00.

Roy Rogers Riders Harmonica by Reed Harmonica Division, c. 1950s. C10–$50.00; C8–$30.00; C6–$15.00; add $50.00 for box.

1953 catalog.

Roy Rogers Signal Siren Flashlight by Usalite, 6" long, with siren whistle at butt end, c. 1950s. C10–$200.00; C8–$150.00; C6–$75.00; add $200.00 for box; add $25.00 for Morse Code Booklet.

Roy Rogers Trail Finder Compass Lite, 6" long, with compass on butt end, c. 1950s. C10–$300.00; C8–$200.00; C6–$100.00; add $250.00 for box.

Roy Rogers Metal Boot Bank, approx. 4½" x 3½" by Fosta Co., rare gold paint version, c. 1950s. C10–$125.00; C8–$75.00; C6–$40.00.
Roy Rogers Metal Boot Bank, copper metal version, same as above. C10–$75.00; C8–$50.00; C6–$25.00.

CREATIVE LONG-PLAYING TOYS

#2160 — Roy Rogers and Dale Evans Western Dress-up Kit
Lifelike figures of Roy and Dale can be "dressed up" in any number of combinations, with fifty-seven colorful plastic stick-on shapes of western clothing to choose from. These no scissors, no paste, no tabs stick-on shapes are interchangeable and can be used over and over. An enclosed booklet illustrates five possible dress-up combinations.
Suggested retail . . . $1.98

#160 — Dale Evans Western Dress-up Kit
Lifelike figure of Dale and a variety of colorful plastic stick-on shapes of outfits for dress-up or riding the range. Illustrated booklet showing several possible combinations is enclosed in the handsome package.
Suggested retail . . . 98¢

#2161 — Roy Rogers Cowboy and Indian Kit
On already-prepared panoramic western workboard, the young cowpoke can create as many scenes as his imagination can dream up by using the plastic stick-on shapes of cowboys, Indians, horses, and many others. With the seventy-two pieces in seven glowing colors, he can picture his own stories of cowboys in camp, Indians on the reservation, or cowboy and Indian wars. An instruction booklet illustrating five typical scenes is included in the big, attractive box.
Suggested retail . . . $1.98

Colorforms
Norwood, N.J.

1959–60 catalog.

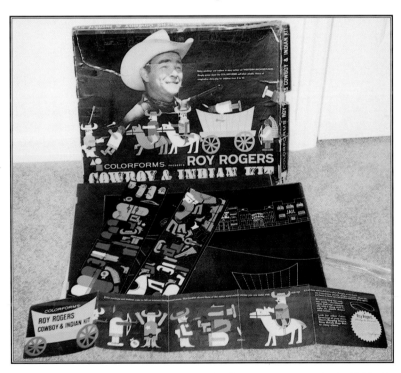

Roy Rogers Cowboy and Indians Colorforms, c. 1950s C10–$200.00; C8–$125.00; C6–$50.00; add $25.00 for original instruction booklet.

NONTOXIC COLORING MATERIALS

#950 — Paint-by-Number Oil Set
Twelve all-plastic vials of oil paints, brushes, palette, two 9" x 12" numbered Roy Rogers pictures, instructions. Fun for all the family.
Suggested retail . . . $2.00
#302RR — Luggage Painting Kit
Poster paints, water colors, crayons, paint brush, outline pictures in luggage carrying case.
Suggested retail . . . $2.00
#301RR — Smaller set . . . $1.00
#947 — Children's Paint-by-Number Set
Water-soluble washable colors with prenumbered pictures featuring Roy Rogers and his pals. Handy instruction booklet, too.
Suggested retail . . . $1.00
#949 — Natural Slate and Chalk Set
Large framed slate for chalk, white on reverse side for whisk-off washable crayons; cutouts; stencils, outline pictures, drawing paper.
Suggested retail . . . $2.00
#948 — Smaller set . . . $1.00
#942RR — Crayon Set
Wrapped crayons, a plastic sharpener, stencils, outline pictures, plus special crayon holders.
Suggested retail . . . $2.00
#941 — Crayon-by-Number Set . . . $1.00
#924 — Modeling Clay Set
Brilliant-colored, never-harden, pliable clay with handy tools, plastic molds, instructions.
Suggested retail . . . $2.00
#923 — Smaller set . . . $1.00

Standard Toykraft Prods., Inc.
95 Lorimer Street
Brooklyn 6, New York

1959–60 catalog.

Roy Rogers Paint Set by Standard Toycraft Prod. Inc., c. 1950s. C10–$250.00; C8–$125.00; C6–$65.00.

Roy Rogers Paint by Numbers Paint Set, c.1950s. C10–$150.00; C8–$75.00; C6–$45.00.

Contents of Marx Set No. 3899. 1959 – 1960 catalog.

Roy Rogers Marx Rodeo
Set No. 3899, box measures 4" x 9" x 22", c. early
1950s.   C10–$400.00;
C8–$200.00; C6–$75.00;

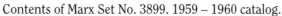

Roy Rogers Marx Rodeo Set, box measures 3½" x 13½" x 15", c. early 1950s.
C10–$400.00; C8–$225.00; C6–$100.00.

Roy Rogers loose Marx Ranch House, part of different version Marx Ranch sets. C10–$75.00; C8–$50.00; C6–$25.00. Double R Gate, $25.00; Nellybelle Jeep, $35.00 from Post cereal premium. Roy and Bullet plastic figures $10.00 each.

Authentically WESTERN
PLAY SETS AND RIFLE

Roy Rogers Mineral City

Miniature replica of Western town. Contains plastic figures of Roy Rogers, Dale Evans, Trigger, Bullet plus 19 cowboys...including bank robber, fist fighter, sheriff...5 plastic horses, 2 calves, Western saddles, fences, trees, buckboard wagon. Metal lithographed building 27½" long, 6" wide, 9" high. A setting for playtime cowboy enjoyment.

Inside of Mineral City buildings are 25 detailed plastic accessories scaled to size — completely furnishes hotel bedroom, music hall, bank, Fargo Express office, barber shop, post office.

Packing : ½ doz. individually boxed sets to flat shipping carton.
Weight : 30 Lbs.
Suggested Retail Price : **$6.00**

1953 catalog.

Roy Rogers loose Marx Mineral City Buildings. C10–$300.00; C8–$150.00; C6–$75.00; add $250.00 for box.

#1420 — Roy Rogers Magic Play-around*
Now youngsters can be their own TV producers. On this magic "play-around" platform, junior cowpokes can put their own stories about Roy Rogers and his exciting adventures into almost-live action. Figures of Roy, Dale Evans, Trigger, Buttermilk — ten in all, decorated realistically on both sides — with magnetic bases, move about with seeming magic in and around a platform set with scenery beautifully lithographed front and back in natural colors on double-thickness board. Four magnets and two guides to work with under the stage allow the youngster plenty of scope for moving his figures about. The scenery and characters are pushouts and set up permanently in three dimensions; the platform, mounted on sturdy legs trimmed with a western rope design, is fully assembled; and all come packed complete in an eye-appealing set-up display box.
Suggested retail . . . $1.98
*U.S. Patents Pending

Amsco Toys
200 Fifth Avenue
New York 10, N.Y.

1959–60 catalog.

Roy Rogers Magic Play Around by Amsco, c. 1950s. C10–$350.00; C8–$225.00; C6–$125.00.

Roy Rogers plastic ball roll game, approx. 3" x 3". C10–$50.00; C8–$35.00; C6–$20.00.

Roy Rogers and Trigger yo-yo in original plastic bag. C10–$30.00; C8–$20.00; C6–$10.00. Many of these have surfaced due to warehouse find.

1953 catalog.

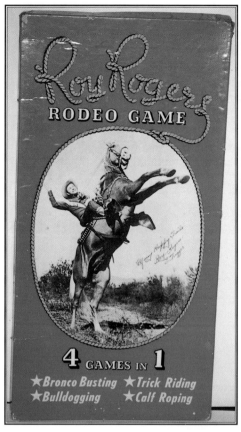

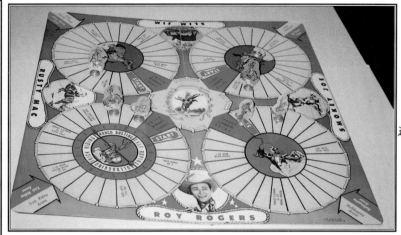

Roy Rogers Rodeo Game by The Rogden Co., c. early 1950s.
C10–$250.00; C8–$125.00; C6–$65.00.

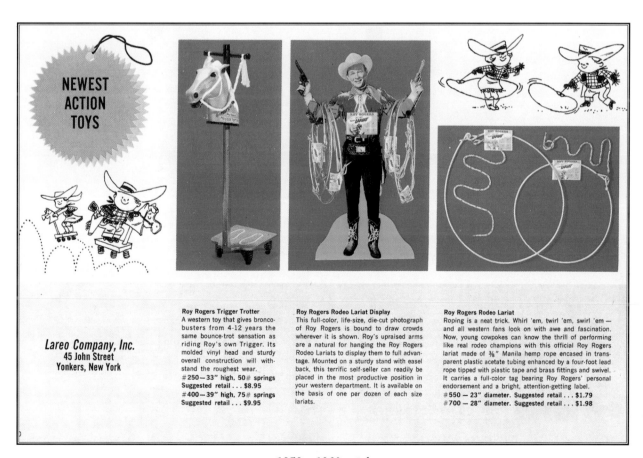

NEWEST ACTION TOYS

Lareo Company, Inc.
45 John Street
Yonkers, New York

Roy Rogers Trigger Trotter
A western toy that gives bronco-busters from 4-12 years the same bounce-trot sensation as riding Roy's own Trigger. Its molded vinyl head and sturdy overall construction will withstand the roughest wear.
#250 — 33" high, 50# springs
Suggested retail . . . $8.95
#400 — 39" high, 75# springs
Suggested retail . . . $9.95

Roy Rogers Rodeo Lariat Display
This full-color, life-size, die-cut photograph of Roy Rogers is bound to draw crowds wherever it is shown. Roy's upraised arms are a natural for hanging the Roy Rogers Rodeo Lariats to display them to full advantage. Mounted on a sturdy stand with easel back, this terrific self-seller can readily be placed in the most productive position in your western department. It is available on the basis of one per dozen of each size lariats.

Roy Rogers Rodeo Lariat
Roping is a neat trick. Whirl 'em, twirl 'em, swirl 'em — and all western fans look on with awe and fascination. Now, young cowpokes can know the thrill of performing like real rodeo champions with this official Roy Rogers lariat made of ⅜" Manila hemp rope encased in transparent plastic acetate tubing enhanced by a four-foot lead rope tipped with plastic tape and brass fittings and swivel. It carries a full-color tag bearing Roy Rogers' personal endorsement and a bright, attention-getting label.
#550 — 23" diameter. Suggested retail . . . $1.79
#700 — 28" diameter. Suggested retail . . . $1.98

1959 – 1960 catalog.

209

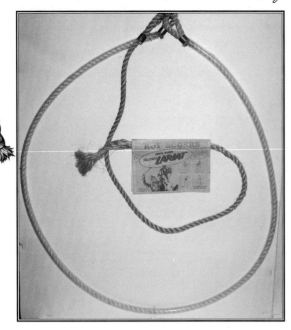

Roy Rogers Rodeo Lariat by Lareo Co., c. 1950s. C10–$150.00; C8–$100.00; C6–$65.00.

Roy Rogers Toy Wagon, approx. 16" x 27". C10–$500.00; C8–$300.00; C6–$200.00; add $100.00 for box.

1959 – 60 catalog.

Roy Rogers Chuck Wagon, missing horse, approx. 18" long. Complete, C10–$300.00; C8–$200.00; C6–$100.00; add $200.00 for box.

Nellybelle, 16" x 20" x 40", long metal pedal car by Sherwood Toys Co., c. 1950s, restored (shown), various colors including gray, dark blue, and light blue. Prices for original C10–$4,000.00; C8–$2,500.00; C6–$750.00. Restored $1,500.00.

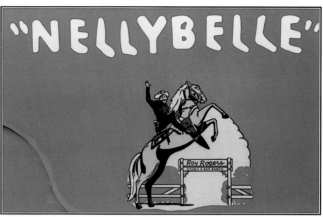

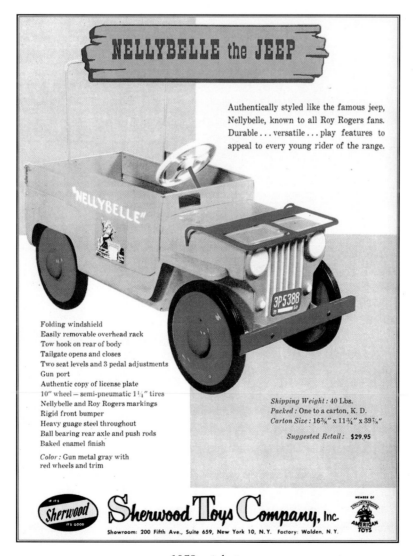

1953 catalog.

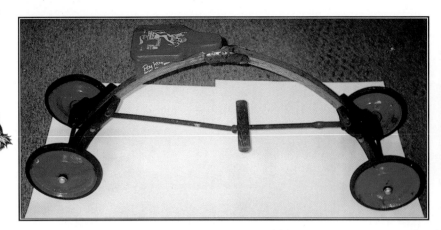

Roy Rogers Hobby Horse by Cass Toys, folds up, missing Trigger's head, rare, c. early 1950s. Complete, C10–$750.00; C8–$350.00; C6–$200.00.

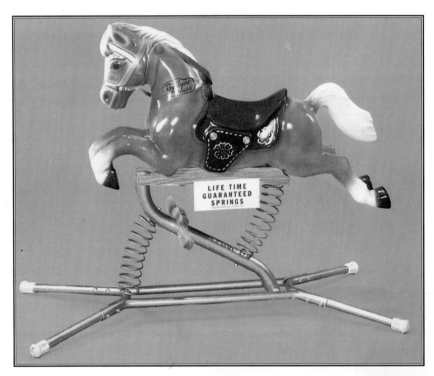

1959 – 60 catalog.

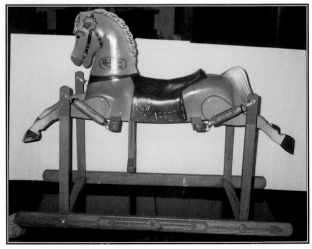

Trigger Spring Horse by Rich Industries Inc., approx. 39" long, c. 1950s. C10–$400.00; C8–$225.00; C6–$100.00.

Trigger Rocking Horse by Trane-Rite Molding Products, approx. 33"l x 10½"w x 24"h., c. 1950s. C10–$300.00; C8–$150.00; C6–$75.00.

Metal and wood Trigger rocking horse. C10–$450.00; C8–$250.00; C6–$125.00.

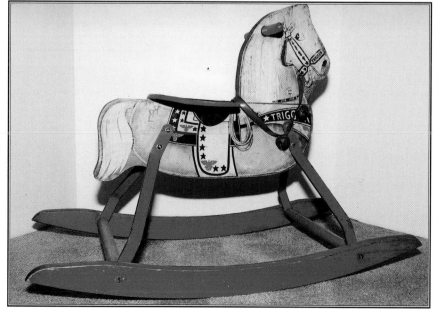

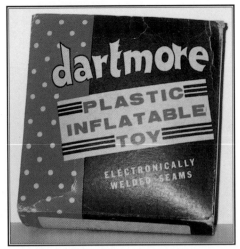

Trigger inflatable toy, 17"h x 21"l, c. 1955.
C10–$200.00; C8–$150.00; C6–$50.00;
add $75.00 for box.

Add $25.00 for original tag on Hart-
land figure.

Roy Rogers Chuck Wagon by Stegel,
1950s, rare. C10–$1,000.00; C8–$500.00;
C6–$250.00.

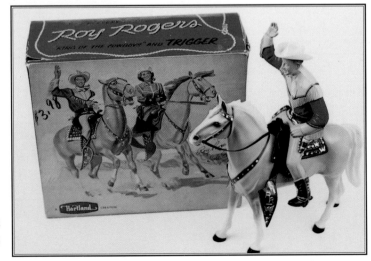

Roy Rogers and Trigger figures by Hartland Plastic
Inc., c. 1950s. Complete, C10–$275.00; C8–$150.00;
C6–$75.00; add $200.00; for 3" x 8" x 9½" box.

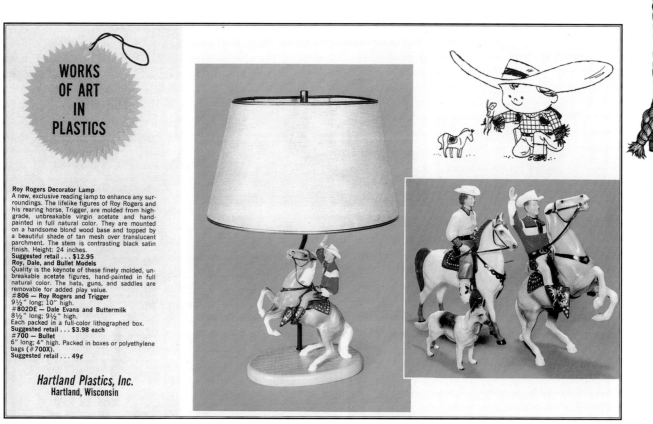

WORKS OF ART IN PLASTICS

Roy Rogers Decorator Lamp
A new, exclusive reading lamp to enhance any surroundings. The lifelike figures of Roy Rogers and his rearing horse, Trigger, are molded from high-grade, unbreakable virgin acetate and hand-painted in full natural color. They are mounted on a handsome blond wood base and topped by a beautiful shade of tan mesh over translucent parchment. The stem is contrasting black satin finish. Height: 24 inches.
Suggested retail ... $12.95
Roy, Dale, and Bullet Models
Quality is the keynote of these finely molded, unbreakable acetate figures, hand-painted in full natural color. The hats, guns, and saddles are removable for added play value.
#806 — Roy Rogers and Trigger
9½" long; 10" high.
#802DE — Dale Evans and Buttermilk
8½" long; 9½" high.
Each packed in a full-color lithographed box.
Suggested retail ... $3.98 each
#700 — Bullet
6" long; 4" high. Packed in boxes or polyethylene bags (#700X).
Suggested retail ... 49¢

Hartland Plastics, Inc.
Hartland, Wisconsin

1959 – 60 catalog. Roy Rogers and Rearing Trigger figures and Hartland Roy Rogers and Rearing Trigger lamp, rare. Lamp, C10–$1,000.00; C8–$500.00; C6–$250.00.

Roy Rogers and Rearing Trigger figures by Hartland Plastic Inc., c. 1950s. Complete, C10–$300.00; C8–$175.00; C6–$100.00; add $200.00 for box.

Dale Evans with green dress and Buttermilk figures by Hartland Plastic Inc., c. 1950s. Complete, C10–$275.00; C8–$150.00; C6–$75.00; add $200.00 for box.

Dale Evans with white blouse and Buttermilk figures by Hartland Plastic Inc., c. 1950s. Complete, C10–$250.00; C8–$125.00; C6–$75.00; add $200.00 for box.

Bullet figure by Hartland Plastic Inc., late 1950s. C10–$150.00; C8–$75.00; C6–$35.00, add $150.00 for box.

Small Roy Rogers figure by Hartland Plastic Inc., c 1950s. C10–$150.00; C8–$100.00; C6–$65.00, add $150.00 for box.

Roy Rogers 32" pressed wood guitar, c.1950s. C10–$350.00; C8–$225.00; C6–$75.00; add $200.00 for original guitar carrying case (not shown).
Roy Rogers 36" pressed wood guitar, c. 1950s. C10–$400.00; C8–$275.00; C6–$100.00; add $200.00 for original guitar carrying case (not shown).

Roy Rogers 30" molded cardboard and wood guitar, by Range Rhythm Toys, c. 1950s. C10–$175.00; C8–$100.00; C6–$50.00; add $150.00 for box.

Roy Rogers 30" molded cardboard and wood guitar by Jefferson Co., also called Sunburst guitar. C10–$175.00; C8–$100.00; C6–$50.00; add $200.00 for box. Notice different version boxes, one with decal that matches guitar other box without decal for different version guitar.

Trigger and Bullet stick horse by N.N. Hill Brass Co., 39"
long. C10–$250.00; C8–$150.00; C6–$75.00.

Roy Rogers and Gabby Hayes 9" tall hand puppets with rubber heads.
C10–$75.00; C8–$45.00; C6–$25.00 each.

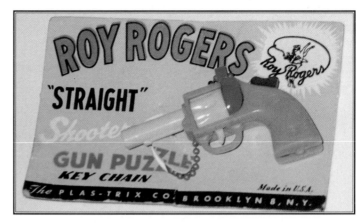

Roy Rogers plastic gun, 3", flashlight. C10–$50.00; C8–$35.00; C6–$20.00.

Straight Shooters Gun Puzzle Key Chain has R initial on handle. Loose C10–$50.00; C8–$35.00; C6–$20.00; add $50.00 for backing card.

Gun Puzzle (same as above with different color), packaged with instructions. C10–$100.00.

Roy Rogers Riders Signal Gun, battery operated, approx. 7" long. C10–$150.00; C8–$100.00; C6–$50.00; add $150.00 for box; add $25.00 for booklet.

Roy Rogers tin litho stopper gun, approx. 9" long, made in Japan, rare. C10–$250.00; C8–$125.00; C6–$75.00.

Roy Rogers View-Master Reels in original View Master sleeves. C10–$15.00; C8–$10.00; C6–$5.00 each.

Roy Rogers Adventure Roundup, 4½" x 4½", View-Master Reels, c. 1956. Complete, C10–$50.00; C8–$35.00; C6–$20.00.

Roy Rogers Tru-Vue three-card album with viewer. Complete, C10–$100.00; C8–$50.00; C6–$25.00.

Roy Rogers, Dale Evans, and Dusty, 11½" x 13" frame tray inlay puzzle, c. 1950s. C10–$50.00; C8–$35.00; C6–$20.00.

Roy Rogers, 11½" x 14½" frame tray inlay puzzle in sleeve, c. 1950s. C10–$50.00; C8–$35.00; C6–$20.00; add $35.00 for sleeve.

Roy Rogers holding gun, 11½" x 13" frame tray inlay puzzle, c. 1950s. C10–$50.00; C8–$35.00; C6–$20.00.

Roy Rogers with Trigger, 11½" x 13" frame tray inlay puzzle, c. 1950s. C10–$50.00; C8–$35.00; C6–$20.00.

Roy Rogers, Trigger, and Bullet, 11½" x 13", frame tray inlay puzzle, c. 1950s. C10–$50.00; C8–$35.00; C6–$20.00.

Roy Rogers standing at saddle, 9½" x 11" frame tray inlay puzzle, c. 1950s. C10–$50.00; C8–$35.00; C6–$20.00.

Roy Rogers with puppies, 9½" x 11" frame tray inlay puzzle, c. 1950s. C10–$50.00; C8–$35.00; C6–$20.00.

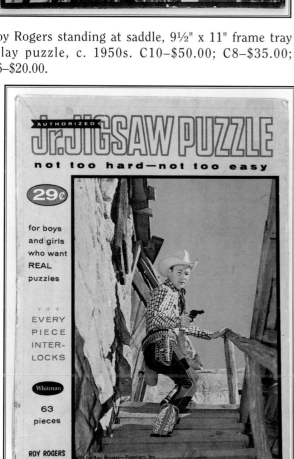

Roy Rogers 7" x 9" boxed junior jigsaw puzzle, c. 1950s. C10–$50.00; C8–$35.00; C6–$20.00.

Roy Rogers, Dale Evans, and Dusty, 7" x 9" boxed junior jigsaw puzzle, c. 1950s. C10–$50.00; C8–$35.00; C6–$20.00

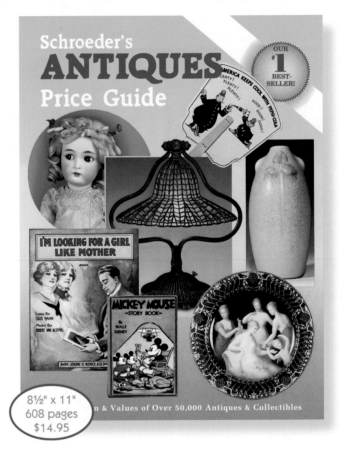